FINALLY, NOW YOU CAN

How to walk in Stability & Resilience, Immovability & Permanence, Possibility & Performance, Restoration & the Halcyon Life

PETER KANGE

outskirts press

Finally, Now You Can
How to Walk in Stability & Resilience, Immovability & Permanence,
Possibility & Performance, Restoration & the Halcyon Life
All Rights Reserved.
Copyright © 2017 Peter Kange
v1.0

The opinions expressed in this manuscript are solely the opinions of the author and do not represent the opinions or thoughts of the publisher. The author has represented and warranted full ownership and/or legal right to publish all the materials in this book.

This book may not be reproduced, transmitted, or stored in whole or in part by any means, including graphic, electronic, or mechanical without the express written consent of the publisher except in the case of brief quotations embodied in critical articles and reviews.

Outskirts Press, Inc.
http://www.outskirtspress.com

ISBN: 978-1-4787-9097-6

Library of Congress Control Number: 2017909656

Cover Photo © 2017 thinkstockphotos.com. All rights reserved - used with permission.

Unless otherwise noted, all Scripture references are from *The Holy Bible*, King James Version (public domain). References marked AMP are from *The Amplified Bible*, copyright © 1987 by the Zondervan Corporation and the Lockman Foundation, La Habra, California.

Outskirts Press and the "OP" logo are trademarks belonging to Outskirts Press, Inc.

PRINTED IN THE UNITED STATES OF AMERICA

Acknowledgment

I acknowledge my LORD and Savior Jesus Christ, who saved me and set me on a path of sanity and purpose; Ma Martha, my pastor and personal confident; Pauline Kange, my wife and partner; and my church family.

Foreword

In an age when proclivities for the extremes are high, this book could not be any timelier. You are about to be exposed to a world of truth that is compelling yet freeing, riveting yet convicting, and seemingly contradictory yet fundamentally simple.

Presented by God through a vessel who experiences and benefits from this, you are sure to encounter Grace, and be completely transformed by Him. You will quickly discover that Grace does not condemn you and does not condone sin either, but rather teaches and empowers you to live triumphantly. The challenges of your life will be demystified, as you will discover in these pages that now, finally you can!

Dig in!

Pauline Kange

Author of *Too Big for Small Things, Too Small for Big Things!*

Dedication

Dear Reader, if I may:

I have laughed, and I have cried. From the days of my humble beginnings to where I can share a lesson or two from life's experiences, I have come to cherish someone as a fantastic partner, constructive critic, and best friend. Knowing much has often impaired many and brought thousands to desert significant relationships BUT not you; rather you got closer. I dedicate this book to you, Pauline Kange. To our incredible sons and daughters, and to you, dear reader. I pray GRACE continues to flow in and through you. May you experience the mysteries of this book's content not only from God but also from those in your life like I have and still do. Keep moving forward; never pause to yield to any circumstance. See you at the award ceremony!

To You and Your Success!

Preface

Many people talk about the "game of life," yet few among the masses understand the rules that govern it or even know there is any such thing. Everyone born of a woman and brought into this world is a recruit by default, and this fact is the very reason why ignorance has become the most deadly of diseases plaguing the very basis of our existence. "To prosper, reproduce, fill the Earth, and take charge! To be responsible for fish in the sea and birds in the air, for every living thing that moves on the face of Earth" (Genesis 1:28).

But how can this be and does this have any real meaning? Could this be even remotely possible or just one of those things that constitute tales and fables? Could one be unconsciously involved in a game or system, and toil days on end only to remain stranded, not understanding what hit them or what they might have done wrong? The answer to all the above questions is YES! Ignorance then becomes a crime punishable by life's hard lessons, which in turn force us to discover our real self, purpose, the rules of the game, and finally, the EMPOWERING FORCE behind every great achievement—GRACE!

The evidence to this MYSTERY lies in our inherent desire for increase. Every living thing continually seeks the enlargement of its life, because life, in the mere act of existence, must improve and continuously adapt itself with the rest of the growing world. The very words of Genesis 1:28 contain within them power and command the same to ensure smooth delivery and success for the human race. One MUST, therefore, seek to UNDERSTAND and MINGLE with the force, GRACE, which empowers each participant of the game of life wherein all systems proceed.

Definitions

I would give this word *grace* a twofold meaning:

1. The power of God that enables you to do all things: saying yes when you need to, and saying no when you need to. Grace is the divine faculty that teaches you to say no to ungodliness and yes to God's will for your life, and also empowers you to execute the same.

2. The unmerited favor of God, the external manifestation of God's power, such as we would find when the Lord confirms His presence or hand upon an individual.

Taking into account these two instances of the intervention of God or grace of God, we could say: Jesus has been made unto us grace (see John 1:14). And, therefore through Christ Jesus, we can do all things. In Luke 1:35 we find that the power of the Highest overshadows, not just to cause the Word to come to pass, but also for the formation of the needed miracle. That is God's grace.

Whenever you hear or think about the word grace as used in this book, think and see the word ABILITY. THINK and SEE the word POSSIBLE. The word GRACE is saying:

There is HELP

You can DO it

You can STAND

You will be a testimony

The door(s) can be opened

You are forgiven

You can RISE AGAIN from any situation

You will WIN, so take the step,

RESTORATION

You can because GRACE did it for you; so, step on in

P.K.

Introduction

As human beings, we are all flawed, and no matter what we do, there will always be a lack of excellence in matters of moral behavior and piety. Such shortcoming stays as part and parcel of each human until God, the Creator of the Universe, joins in and changes us. For believers and unbelievers alike, He has made provision for us to experience redemption through His ability, His amazing grace at work in us. As a result, we can declare, with the apostle Paul:

I can do all things through Christ which strengtheneth me. **Philippians 4:13**

Yes, I am weak, but He is strong, and through Him, I can achieve excellence in my daily life. We are not destined just to end with the knowledge of God's grace, but to go beyond, and by faith, to reach out for its application in our daily lives. God wants to work with each of us and in all areas of our lives, regardless of the circumstance or situation. He has made provision for an escape from the pressure to quit or give up in the face of life's challenges and a progression toward total victory.

As we step out in faith, His power is unveiled with every step, crying, "Grace! Grace!" unto every mountain on our path unleashing divine enablement. This grace is not just for me to stand in the face of the challenge but also the grace to cause every mountain to move, and the deployment of external help through human agents and/or natural elements such as the wind, rain, and sun as needed. Without Christ, I am not enough, or better said, I am nothing. With Him, however, I am complete, and all things are possible to me. That's God's grace at work in my life. Therefore, I shout, *Grace! Grace!*

Peter Kange

Beltsville, Maryland

Table of Contents

"It is grace at the beginning, and grace at the end. So that when you and I come to lie upon our deathbeds, the one thing that should comfort and help and strengthen us there is the thing that helped us in the beginning. Not what we have been, not what we have done, but the Grace of God in Jesus Christ our Lord. The Christian life starts with grace, it must continue with grace, it ends with grace. Grace, wondrous grace. By the grace of God I am what I am. Yet not I, but the Grace of God which was with me."

— David Lloyd-Jones

CHAPTER 1

Grace! Grace! The Way Out

Then the angel that talked with me answered and said unto me, Knowest thou not what these be? And I said, No, my lord. Then he answered and spake unto me, saying, This is the Word of the Lord unto Zerubbabel, saying, Not by might, nor by power, but by My spirit, saith the Lord of hosts. Who art thou, O great mountain? Before Zerubbabel thou shalt become a plain: and he shall bring forth the headstone thereof with shoutings, crying, Grace, grace unto it. **Zechariah 4:5-7**

And when he came to him, behold, he stood by his burnt offering, and the princes of Moab with him. And Balak said unto him, What hath the Lord spoken? And he took up his parable, and said, Rise up, Balak, and hear; hearken unto me, thou son of Zippor: God is not a man, that he should lie; neither the son of man, that he should repent: hath he said, and shall he not do it? Or hath he spoken, and shall he not make it good? **Numbers 23:17-19**

God is not a man that He should lie. He doesn't say one thing to-day and something different tomorrow. People are prone to chang-ing their minds, but we serve a God who never changes His. If He said a thing, then it *will* come to pass, and you can count on it. Oh, what an amazing truth! This reality means that everything you are about to read will increase awareness and stir up the faith required for His promises coming to pass. It will not happen by the might or power of men, but by the workings of the Spirit of the Lord. We have heard stories of people fired from companies they worked for and then, only a few years later, they are invited to come back and teach others at the same workplace on leadership. Can you imag-ine that? Can you imagine an organization that fired you on the grounds of incompetence and did not think you were worth $30 an hour calling you back, with an offer of $30,000 an hour to give a speech or to implement an employee improvement training pro-gram? Now, that's amazing!

Typically, that is what happens when the grace of God is at work in and through you. Open yourself up for miracles as you are go-ing through the pages of this book; the mountain before you will soon become flat land. That *will* come to pass. Stop trying to live an overly cautious life full of fear and no daring, and step into the overflow of God's grace, because that is your portion.

The first credit card ever issued to me had a limit of only $300. Spending that amount was way easier than getting it paid off. I struggled to pay the balance. At times, I would overdraw the limit, and the creditors will come calling at the most unexpected periods of the day. When I think back on those days, I wonder: Was God just encouraging me? How is it possible that I could not manage to pay $300? But that was the reality. Those were the days of small beginnings. As God's children, we should be able to smile as we pay a $25,000 bill or a $300 bill. I now know that regardless of what I am facing, it is to my advantage to go through with joy. It is the same God releasing the same grace on both sides of the spectrum. That is why I love hearing testimonies of people making transfers of massive amounts of money. If the mountain before you is one of debt, it is about to become a plain in Jesus' name. Receiving a Word at a low point in life is just what makes the difference between going through with joy or sadness. At one point, I got just that from my pastor, who said to me, "This is the lowest you will ever be." Hearing those words gave me such a lift and an assurance that not only will all be well but also an awareness that I was not going through alone. I was so happy about this news that I skipped for joy. Today, I declare the same thing to you: This is the lowest point you will ever be. Start your upward climb from this moment on, by God's grace.

The Power of Vision

As we look at many countries around the world, the United States of America (being one of them) seems to stand out because it has great vision. Have you ever noticed how long the U.S. social security numbers are? That's because visionaries anticipated how many citizens they would one day have to track. When American engineers are doing road construction, they often construct an alternate route or a temporary road to be used as they put together the permanent one. At the end of the work project, the road that served as a detour for traffic is then dug off and replaced with beautiful fresh grass. It takes vision for all of this to be effective. Such attention to detail and a future-based mindset are the reasons behind uncommon progression in certain people who can go beyond the norm. Vision helps you see possibilities. The power and/or grace within a vision will enable you to fulfill whatever task you have at hand, no matter who you are or your origin.

As you may have noticed, I am using *grace* and *power* interchangeably. Vision is so potent that it releases power to its bearer, enabling them to do the impossible. It will be hard for you to experience grace if there is nothing as in a task or assignment with which to experiment. Step out, and you will be amazed at the power that is already available for you to succeed.

I wonder what life would be like in this beautiful world we live in, if every nation and its leadership stopped every endeavor and began a new type of culture-shaping by modeling every agenda from a place of vision.

Our Future in God Is Bright

God has promised us the blessing:

Behold, I have received commandment to bless: and he hath blessed; and I cannot reverse it. He hath not beheld iniquity in Jacob, neither hath he seen perverseness in Israel: the Lord his God is with him, and the shout of a king is among them. God brought them out of Egypt; he hath as it were the strength of an unicorn. Surely there is no enchantment against Jacob, neither is there any divination against Israel: according to this time it shall be said of Jacob and of Israel, What hath God wrought! **Numbers 23:20-23**

As believers in the Lord Jesus and His Word, of course, we inherit these promises, though their manifestation requires our awareness and faith. God wants to use you so that somebody can look stupid; I know very well how foolish it sounds to those who are lost as it did to me at one point when they hear that Jesus died to save them. But we who are already experiencing His saving grace recognize this message as the very power of God. He wants to change your story so that those who laugh at you will come to you for advice. The Word of God assures us that He wants to make us *"a praise in the earth"* (Isaiah 62:7).

You know how it is when you go to church and tell the preacher that you have a testimony to give? Well, God wants to make you and me the testimony. The promise from the Word of God is that no enchantment nor divination will work against us because of the shout of the King. If that roar is really in your camp, you need to be screaming it out, and according to Zechariah 4:7, we won't just be shouting meaningless words, but we will be shouting "Grace! Grace!" That is because our victory comes by God's grace.

Many consider themselves to be weak and incapable. Many feel as if they didn't go to school nearly long enough. But God is saying that you are capable. I want you to take a minute and meditate on all of this and then speak it out loud to your hearing—I am able to do all things and experience all things by the grace of God. Considering the scriptural passages we have just looked at, I want you to set before you everything that troubles your heart and then just shout "Grace" to it. Shout "Grace" to that which troubles you, releasing the roar of the King—the Lion of the tribe of Judah—to that circumstance. Just take a minute and yell: "Grace! Grace!"

The Grace of God Is Supernatural

What's so powerful about those words: Grace! Grace!? The grace of God is supernatural. The Bible tells us that God had mercy on Israel, as a manifestation of His grace. Mercy is one of the components that reveals grace, the other two being goodness and favor. In manifestation of this truth that His goodness endures forever, He split the Red Sea and led them across. As a result of His goodness and mercy toward Israel, He killed all of the Egyptians. On account of His goodness and mercy toward His children, He gave them all the riches of the Egyptians. And owing to His continued goodness and mercy, God will transfer wealth from the wicked to you. He will destroy the wicked for you. This is the lowest you will ever be, according to His grace. Begin your upward climb today.

"I Will Heal Their Land"

God wants to heal our land, and for us to understand the fullness or vastness of this statement and promise, we need to define the word *land*. Firstly: In economics, land comprises all naturally occurring resources whose supply is inherently fixed. Examples are any and all particular geographical locations, mineral deposits, forests, fish stocks, atmospheric quality, geostationary orbits, and portions of the electromagnetic spectrum.

Secondly: In business, land is real estate or property, minus buildings and equipment, that does not occur in a natural way. Land ownership may offer the title holder the right to natural resources on the land. The traditional school of economics dictates that land is a factor of production, *along with capital and labor.*

God's Word declares:

If my people, which are called by my name, shall humble themselves, and pray, and seek my face, and turn from their wicked ways; then will I hear from heaven, and will forgive their sin, and will heal their land. **2 Chronicles 7:14**

When we come into a place of alignment with the laws of God, we make way for the grace of God to come in and not only aid us, but also heal our land. It is by grace that God is able to forgive, and by the same grace, He heals. At no time is this made more evident that His grace is a compilation of goodness, mercy, and favor. Oh yes, He will forgive us and heal our land. Come therefore to the Lord, draw nigh expecting to find grace to help in time of need. He who has not only power over but also created everything that is will forgive; throwing away or discarding the reason for sickness in our land and bringing healing to it. When God forgives, healing follows (also see Luke 5:20-24 and Psalm 103:3). If sin can be forgiven, then healing will come without fail. He will heal geographical locations, mineral deposits, forests, fish stocks, atmospheric quality, geostationary orbits, and portions of the electromagnetic spectrum. Hallelujah!

Redeeming the Land

When we talk about land, what comes to mind? It is a place where I can plant and harvest, right? Whether you describe "land" as a country (state, nation, home) or as property (area or estate) or as an agent of production (field or farm), the meaning is straight-forward. From Genesis onward, fish were bred in the sea, and there they had their existence. We, however, are made from the ground, and we eat from the ground. But do you realize that when Adam and Eve fell, the thing that was cursed was the very ground they had come from and which sustained them? In Galatians, however, we are told that we have been *"redeemed... from the curse of the law"* **(Galatians 3:13).** In other words, the ground should now pro-duce for you and me.

God has said, *"If my people, which are called by my name, shall humble themselves... then will I... heal their land"* **(2 Chronicles 7:14)**. When Adam and Eve sinned, the entire human race fell with them, but when we give our lives to Jesus (with the heart one be-lieves, resulting in righteousness, and with the mouth confession is made, resulting in salvation), we are redeemed from that curse. One thing the first Adam never did was return to God and ask Him for healing for the land, BUT we can do that today from the re-demptive provision of the cross.

The situation is similar with the woman. She can recognize that God's Word says there will be an increase in pain in childbirth, but she can also remind Him that she is not Eve. She has been saved by Jesus, and as a result, she is the resurrected Eve, who has no such word as *pain* in her vocabulary.

In the same way, the Word of God tells us that in the last days the knowledge of the glory of God will increase to the point that it will be as the waters covering the seas **(Habakkuk 2:14)**. The knowledge of God's redemption in our lives will increase. The more knowledge you get, the more grace is made available to you. The more you increase in God's Word, the more you will increase in miracles. This is how God will heal our land. Adam had to toil before he ate. In our dispensation, because we have Christ's blood, shed on the cross, and we are receiving the redemptive work of God, that curse has passed, and we can walk into God's favor as never before.

The Word of God makes us understand, in 1 Peter 2:10, that we were not a people, but now we are the people of God. We had no identity. We were aliens. Many are citizens of one country or another, but as far as the Bible is concerned, if you don't know Jesus, you are an alien. When we come to know Jesus, we are engrafted into the Beloved, and now, as children of the House, our Father is telling us to humble ourselves.

The Need for Humility

Some time ago while having a conversation with my pastor one early morning, she shared with me the wisdom behind a decision she had just made. She let go of her right to be right and took on a humble position, saying, "Let the Lord deal with it as He sees fit." I was thrown off, because in my logical mind at the time, the ball was in her court and she could curb it as she saw fit. In our conversation and many more after that, she would often say, "The Spirit of God does not strive. It is an honor for a man to keep away from strife by handling situations with thoughtful foresight, but any fool will start a quarrel without regard for the consequences. Every contention has an expiration date; my son be at peace this fuss will come to an end."

You see, the topic of grace and humility is such an intriguing one. Grace will not fit into anyone's mold yet invites all humans everywhere to come in and fit into its mold. Humility then is that heart condition that a human takes in acknowledgment of God and His sovereign will. Humility is saying, "I yield to you, Lord, now and forever, whenever and for whatever reason you might require me."

The opposite of humility will be rebellion. This word is used to describe an attempt to topple the government; a plot to overthrow the ruling party, be it in a political, family, or job setting. Such an endeavor requires a fight. Please consider for a minute what it will look like if you or a child you know stands and begins to fight the nurses or doctors who want to infuse them with medication using a syringe. Until there is calm and the fight stops, no one can help the situation. God is ready with a syringe filled up with grace; if you would just yield, you would, without fail, experience a surge of grace infused into your world.

The Lord led me to this scripture to demonstrate to me the power of yielding and waiting upon Him.

Even the youths shall faint and be weary, and the young men shall utterly fall: but they that wait upon the Lord shall renew their strength; they shall mount up with wings as eagles; they shall run, and not be weary; and they shall walk, and not faint. **Isaiah 40:30-31**.

God began telling me that when we take a humbling position, He strengthens us. I began to see, in the eyes of my spirit, someone who was down, waiting for God to help them. As this waiting process progressed, something within them, which looked like a generator of sorts, started forming strength in them. In the process of time, this generator amassed such a surge of energy. God, who is the master over every doorway, knows the duration of your wait time. In time with a little more patience, you will not only hear the cracking of a door, but see your next door opening wide before you. This is God causing you to shoot forth or rise up like a rocket, out of the surge of power, just as the Word tells us:

As arrows are in the hand of a mighty man; so are children of the youth.
Psalm 127:4

As we humble ourselves and wait on God, He is preparing us, and He is formulating us for a precise target. In the days to come, people will come to you and ask you the secret to your success. They want to know what mechanics sustains your performance. It will be because of the strength inside of you, and that strength is from no one but God. It is His grace at work.

Listen and Obey

Hear the Father's lament:

If my people would but listen to me, if Israel would follow my ways.
Psalm 81:13

Obedience is another word for humility. For you to experience the grace of God, you have to be a listener. The one who is disposed to listen and obey is always positioned to flow with grace. Why was He saying this to the children of Israel? Because too often we look to things or people rather than to God. And when God speaks to us about redemptive strategies, we choose to listen to those who communicate to us the state of affairs—our bonds. They tell us that we are bound, while God is saying that we are free. This was the reason, in Exodus, that God began to address Pharaoh directly and to tell him to let the Israelites go:

And the Lord said unto Moses, Rise up early in the morning, and stand before Pharaoh; lo, he cometh forth to the water; and say unto him, Thus saith the Lord, Let my people go, that they may serve me. Else, if thou wilt not let my people go, behold, I will send swarms of flies upon thee, and upon thy servants, and upon thy people, and into thy houses: and the houses of the Egyptians shall be full of swarms of flies, and also the ground whereon they are. **Exodus 8:20-21**

It is about time that you and I wake up in the morning, stand outside, and speak to the wind, the clouds, and the ground and command them to favor us, to prosper us, and to make us the best wherever we go and in everything we do. Some Egyptians are about to call on God because of your prayers. Calamity will suddenly come to their families and to their houses and lands, and they will release you from whatever shackles with which you have been enslaved.

You Are the Boss

Let me ask you something: Why should someone have the right to fire you (especially in an instance of prejudice) just because they happen to be your boss? As much as they have the authority to fire you, you, on the other hand, have a voice as a child of God and the Word of God on your side to call on your Father for intervention. In the Spirit realm, you are the boss. You have the Word of God behind you. If someone is trying to wrongfully terminate you, just release a word about their ground not producing and yours producing, and it will come to pass.

What about the one who deserves to be fired or terminated? I am happy you asked! Yes, that is the reason for this book. He qualifies and fights for the undeserving, who will acknowledge Him as Lord. Oh, beloved, we are only beginning to understand the wonders available to us through God's grace. Shout it today: *Grace! Grace!*

"Soar back through all your own experiences. Think of how the Lord has led you in the wilderness and has fed and clothed you every day. How God has borne with your ill manners, and put up with all your murmurings and all your longings after the 'sensual pleasures of Egypt!' Think of how the Lord's grace has been sufficient for you in all your troubles."

– Charles Spurgeon

CHAPTER 2

The Mind of Grace

In this chapter, we will explore the role of our thought processes and how we can work the path of grace. Aligning our thoughts to the Word of God is of prime importance, coupled with ingesting the mind of God. This combination is the bedrock and landing strip for His grace.

"For as [a man] thinketh in his heart, so is he." **Proverbs 23:7**

What is the mind? It is the seat of intellect and reason; the element of a person that enables them to be aware of the world and their experiences, to think, and to feel; the faculty of consciousness and thought. The mind of grace is therefore birthed out of recurring bricks as in line upon line, precept upon precept of grace-words. To think or to have the Spirit of grace is to harness the concept of grace in one's mind; it is to wear grace as a cloak. Considering that the mind of grace isn't inherent in us, then a walk in righteousness (being on the same page with God or grace), is equally unnatural.

As it is written, There is none righteous, no, not one. **Romans 3:10**

Grace is provided for us so that we can access righteousness freely, and by doing this, we access, embody, and transport God Himself. The Word of God tells us:

He that believeth on me, as the scripture hath said, out of his belly shall flow rivers of living water. **John 7:38**

Now, these rivers do not flow without a source. They emanate from a person, and that Person is none other than Jesus Himself, residing within you. The work of Jesus inside of you takes place by you believing His Word according to His standard. Unquestionably so, God wants to flow through you and me as rivers, not just in splashes and spills, but in a great gushing manner. Paul wrote to the Romans:

There is none that understandeth, there is none that seeketh after God. **Romans 3:11**

"There is none that understandeth." If you lose your grace, your standing or position of righteousness, you will also lose your understanding. The righteousness that we receive by faith through Jesus Christ also causes us to come to a place of understanding.

"There is none that seeketh after God." Without this deposit of the righteousness of God, there is no natural tendency on our part to seek God. The mind of grace is cultivated as we understand righteousness.

Paul continued:

They are all gone out of the way, they are together become unprofitable; there is none that doeth good, no, not one. **Romans 3:12**

The Mind of Grace

The righteous life is "the way." God's "way" is the way of righteousness. This way is altogether made possible only by GRACE!

Taking a Step Back

Let us take a step back and look at the patriarch Abraham and Noah, as someone who walked in the mind of grace.

Even as Abraham believed God, and it was accounted to him for righteousness. **Galatians 3:6**

Abraham's righteousness was not of himself. It was a result of God's grace activated by Abraham's faith. Hearing the voice of God asking him to leave all he knew, into a future he was utterly clueless about, required that Abraham forfeit the right to "think things through." He believed, he stepped out, and through this daring move, he walked into the grace of God. Grace led him to battles and victories and gave him the wisdom, courage, and boldness to forge forward in the face of uncertainties.

We are also told of the man named Noah who walked by faith, and as a result of his faith walk, the world was condemned:

By faith Noah, being warned of God of things not seen as yet, moved with fear, prepared an ark to the saving of his house; by the which he condemned the world, and became heir of the righteousness which is by faith. **Hebrews 11:7**

It is a great challenge to believe in something you cannot see. To do that, your belief must rest not on what you are seeing (or, in this case, not seeing), but on Who is telling you about what you are yet to see. Noah's belief was resting upon the One who had talked with him. The Bible then says, *"...moved with fear, [he] prepared an ark to the saving of his house; by the which, he condemned the world..."* Noah believed God, and his belief condemned the world. Never minimize your faith. The Word of God says that it has *"great recompense of reward"* (Hebrews 10:35). Your faith can be the yardstick for which a building burns, as in the case of Sodom and Gomorrah or the people in Noah's day, because it became the standard God used to bring judgment.

When God visited Noah and told him about the coming flood, remember that it had never rained before upon the earth. This fact never created a platform for absurdity in his mind; Noah had never seen rain, yet he continued his preparations and construction of the Ark because God had said it would rain. Accepting this Word from the Lord as an absolute reality tendered in Noah a walk in the mind of grace. Our walk of faith is not based on what we see. Our walk of faith is an act of worship—an unquestionable loyalty, marinated in obeisance toward God and to His sovereign will.

Abraham Offered What He Loved Most

What does the Bible tell us about Abraham's trip to the mountain to offer his son Isaac? It says:

And Abraham said unto his young men, Abide ye here with the ass; and I and the lad will go yonder and worship, and come again to you. **Genesis 22:5**

Notice this word *worship.* Do you realize that this was an act of faith on Abraham's part? When you are able to take heed of the voice of God concerning the impossible and then walk in it as well, it is because you have cultivated the mind of grace. Do not let anything take you out of this fashion because it is through this method that your miracles come. The mind of grace says to the impossible: "Nothing in the natural indicates to me that I will go through, but I believe in the One who said it. Because He said it, I know that it will come to pass." And it always does.

"He Passed Judgment"

The Amplified Bible renders the last part of Hebrews 11:7 this way:

By this [his faith which relied on God] he passed judgment and sentence on the world's unbelief and became an heir and possessor of righteousness (that relation of being right into which God puts the person who has faith).

Hold on for a minute! Who *"passed ... the sentence"* here? Wasn't it God who brought the flood? That's what we have always believed, right? But see what the Word says here. It says: *"he [Noah] passed judgment and sentence on the world's unbelief."* Your act of worship out of a mindset of faith will get someone in trouble with the courts of heaven, if they're not careful. I'm telling you that you and I are walking bombs. We are going about with the judgment and sentence of God behind our very behavior. That's the reason people get fired from their jobs when you believe what God has told you. As a result of your belief, someone gets ejected so that you can be injected. Your faith has brought about judgment and sentence on that oppressor.

What does this tell us? No one is strong enough to oppose the Lord, who is on your side and working on your behalf. No matter who it is, because of your faith and trust, coupled with unquestionable loyalty and soaked in reverence towards Him and His sovereign Word, they will be brought down. That is why we need to know how to pray, and channel our prayers with the consciousness of grace mixed with faith. Pressing on in faith will cause whatever or whoever we meet along the way to yield to our judgment and sentence. There is judgment in our operation, and we will judge and pass sentence on others as we walk in faith.

God Is Building a People Who Understand Grace

In these last days, God is developing a community of individuals who comprehend His grace, which resides inside of them. They understand their position as a child of God and know that it holds more weight than the circumstances of the world. God in His Word used Sarah to exemplify the timeless nature of His intervention in our lives. He is bringing to our attention the fact that we can give birth at any age, rise again after a fall, and become what nature has told us we can't. Abraham, Sarah's husband, is also used to show us that we can come from nothing to wealth, we may abandon all yet possess much later, be dead and yet, by grace, become alive. It is not the world's standards that count, but God's standards. The covenant between God and Abraham had God exchanging His fruitfulness with Abraham's unfruitfulness, and as a result, Abraham became profitable. When righteousness was accounted to him, he suddenly received understanding and was on his way to prosperity.

God, by His Word and by experience, is teaching the wonders of grace and bringing many to the untold mysteries of the gospel; depicting the power made available through the death and resurrection of Jesus Christ, our Lord.

Our Righteousness in God

By faith, he sojourned in the land of promise, as in a strange country, dwelling in tabernacles with Isaac and Jacob, the heirs with him of the same promise. **Hebrews 11:9**

When the Lord God chose Abraham for a covenant relationship and to establish him as the father of faith, it was necessary for Abraham to leave his previous life and walk into the new. God was making sure that the things He was getting ready to do in Abraham's life gave glory to no one else but Himself.

Now the Lord had said unto Abram, Get thee out of thy country, and from thy kindred, and from thy father's house, unto a land that I will shew thee. **Genesis 12:1**

Abraham did it because it was God's way, and his obedience earned him the title and position of "father of faith." Through him, we now have a better covenant. Now it is written, in Romans 3:10, *"There is none righteous, no, not one,"* yet when you and I accept Jesus, we become the righteous ones of God with understanding;

21

people who seek God and are on their way to total victory. Through Abraham, you and I became profitable.

God said:

Beloved, I wish above all things that thou mayest prosper and be in health, even as thy soul prospereth. **3 John 1:2**

The word *prosper* here is the same word used for *profiting.* Even as Joshua 1:8 teaches us*:*

This book of the law shall not depart out of thy mouth; but thou shalt meditate therein day and night, that thou mayest observe to do according to all that is written therein: for then thou shalt make thy way prosperous, and then thou shalt have good success. **Joshua 1:8**

You and I profit out of righteousness and the mind of grace.

Converted Minds

Righteousness isn't just our state and stance as children of God in the realm of the spirit, from the standpoint of the finished work of the cross; it is how our thoughts become products of the mind of grace. No wonder the Word of God declares:

Let this mind be in you, which was also in Christ Jesus. **Philippians 2:5**

Let it happen. Permit the mind of Christ to settle within and overtake your soul. Once this mind absorbs your mind, you will be in understanding, and you will be ready to profit. Remember the Parable of the Talents? Jesus spoke there of an *"unprofitable servant"*:

And cast ye the unprofitable servant into outer darkness: there shall be weeping and gnashing of teeth. **Matthew 25:30**

Why was this man unremunerated? It was because he refused the mind of Christ, and that cost him profitability. Every single time you step away from righteousness, you become very unproductive, especially as pertaining to the Kingdom of God. When we consider the kingdom of heaven to be a spiritual place that operates with spiritual principles, it takes our concept of the mind's value to a whole new level. The kingdoms of darkness and light both operate with the use of words for either creating good or evil. Things come into being because they have been spoken into formation. Having the right frame of mind is therefore pragmatic to an effective and well-directed, creative tongue. A mind saturated with the Word of God will most definitely direct its proprietors' conversation as the oracles of God.

The man in Matthew 25:30 lost perspective of the Master's intentions and accused him rather than take responsibility and act in a similar manner as the others who invested their talents.

"Lord, I knew thee that thou art an hard man, reaping where thou hast not sown, and gathering where thou hast not strawed: and I was afraid, and went and hid thy talent in the earth: lo, there thou hast that is thine." **Matthew 25:24-25**

This angered his Lord because the mind of grace not only sets us on a path to produce but also renders unto us the mindset of the

Master; which in turn keeps us from a hazardous life of unprofit-ability—weeping and gnashing of teeth:

"His lord answered and said unto him, Thou wicked and slothful servant, thou knewest that I reap where I sowed not, and gather where I have not strawed: thou oughtest therefore to have put my money to the exchang-ers, and then at my coming I should have received mine own with usury. **Matthew 25:26-27**

Notice how his Master rebuked him in verse 27; more like some-one who had lost their mind, his decision was no longer sensible. Tell me, who buries money in the ground? This man was no longer thinking clearly. This was the result of the lack of proper basis for right thinking, which is the revelation of the Word of the Master. Assimilating foreign concepts deprived him from the way of under-standing. In the book of Isaiah we are told that anyone who is will-ing and obedient will eat the good of the land. This is an indication that when anyone is disposed to obey before an instruction is given, they turn to act instantly, without pondering or asking questions.

When you become born again and are made righteous, your mind takes a little while to catch up with your new nature in Christ and old patterns gradually disintegrate. As a result, you may still have traces of the unbeliever or unrighteous person you used to be. A behavior change then requires the child of God to walk in the light of God's Word in obedience and submission. So we are lying if we say we have fellowship with God but go on living in spiritual darkness; we are not practicing the truth. But if we are living in the light, as God is in the light, then we have fellowship with each other, and the blood of Jesus, his Son, not only cleanses us from all sin but also does a perfect work of pruning.

Let me bring your attention to what the well-known Psalm 23 says:

Yea, though I walk through the valley of the shadow of death, I will fear no evil: for thou art with me; thy rod and thy staff they comfort me. **Psalm 23:4**

There is no way a rod or staff can bring consolation, at least not to the flesh, because rods or staffs are meant to bring correction or chastisement. So what did David mean here? How will a rod and staff bring comfort? Well, that will happen while God is leading you beside still waters and restoring your soul. This experience is described by Jesus as pruning:

I am the true vine, and my Father is the husbandman. Every branch in me that beareth not fruit he taketh away: and every branch that beareth fruit, he purgeth it, that it may bring forth more fruit. **John 15:1-2**

While God is feeding you, He is also trimming you and eradicating all anti-enhancing and self-destructive agents from your system. Such pruning may affect certain things we so dearly cherish, such as friends, family, habits, social beliefs, political views, and more, yet it is essential for better performance. That is when His rod and staff give you comfort for all that you have lost. (Take note that the purpose of the rod and staff is not just for leading the sheep. They were also used to cause miracles to happen for them.) Whenever the loss of things happens, the rod and staff also bring about redirection; one form of life is over with, and it is time for another to come into play. As it happened with Elijah, when the brooks dry up, seasons switch, and it is time to be fed by the widow. Pay attention to every loss, and tune in to the direction and leading of the rod and staff of the Good Shepherd, The LORD JESUS.

Good Works Follow

Our covenant relationship with the Lord, procured by the finished work on the cross, not only gave us access to heaven but also included multiplication of every area of our lives; He came to give us life and that, more abundantly. When we begin to manifest profitability, we have attained a status that enables us to naturally birth good works. Remember, again, what Romans 3:12 has said: *"They are all gone out of the way, they are together become unprofitable; there is none that doeth good, no, not one."* Three things are magnified in the above verse:

1. **The way**: This is the path of righteousness; the designated direction for our God-given destiny. It is the path we must follow if we will ever benefit from the grace of God. Anything less will be considered a place of toiling, weeping, and gnashing of teeth. The way is, therefore, that place in which the hand and ability of God flow at a constant pace. This way is narrow and winding but it is the way of the kingdom, and it brings much profit.

2. **Profitability**: This is the place of bestowed benefits; the merits that come from not just following, but also being a good steward. It is the place called abundance, the dwelling of the willing and obedient; the home of the mature, lowly, and meek.

3. **Doing good**: Oh, what a blessing to experience this place! Very few find this station of honor and service. When you attain this level, you no longer live for yourself but for others. At this juncture, your life is poured out for others in graceful service.

Jesus experienced this in His life and ministry. Though He was a Son, these different aspects manifested in His life. No shortcuts, no favoritism, no escaping from the process of molding on the way to success. Once Jesus was anointed, something interesting happened—He went about doing good.

How God anointed Jesus of Nazareth with the Holy Ghost and with power: who went about doing good, and healing all that were oppressed of the devil; for God was with him. **Acts 10:38**

The more of the grace of God we experience, the more we are inclined to be a blessing to others. We want to do good because good has been shown to us. The flow of the anointing is perfected when there is an absolute alignment. This alignment says we are on the same page with the Father. We are in a place or position of righteousness. There is nothing more beautiful than walking in righteousness; it brings with it a sense of peace, boldness, and the courage to confront life. We can only access such right standing with God by the grace of God and through faith in our Lord Jesus Christ. The prophet Isaiah declared:

Until the Spirit be poured upon us from on high, and the wilderness be a fruitful field, and the fruitful field be counted for a forest. Then judgment shall dwell in the wilderness, and righteousness remain in the fruitful field. And the work of righteousness shall be peace; and the effect of righteousness quietness and assurance for ever. **Isaiah 32:15-17**

Are you ready for fruitfulness? The Father has not only made you fruitful, but He has made fruit bearing a thing of ease. Open your heart, get ready, become aware of the baskets made available to collect the harvest, and reach out, for there is a deluge of fruits coming your way, and this is well pleasing to the Lord.

"It Shall Come to Pass"

The writings of the Old Testament come alive as we walk down the pages of the New Testament. It is quite thrilling seeing the fulfillment of prophecy. We either read, "It shall come to pass," or "It came to pass." Clearly, the Old Testament concealed the New Testament, while the New Testament reveals the Old Testament. One such occurrence is seen in the book of Joel in this marvelous declaration:

And it shall come to pass afterward, that I will pour out my spirit upon all flesh; and your sons and your daughters shall prophesy, your old men shall dream dreams, your young men shall see visions: and also upon the servants and upon the handmaids in those days will I pour out my spirit. And I will shew wonders in the heavens and in the earth, blood, and fire, and pillars of smoke. The sun shall be turned into darkness, and the moon into blood, before the great and terrible day of the Lord come. **Joel 2:28-31**

These words of prophecy came alive after the death of Jesus and reveal today the trait marks of the redeemed church of God. The events of Acts 2 then speak loudly of not only a move of the Spirit but also attest to the fact that Jesus died, was buried and resurrected to complete the salvation plan of the Father. Acts Chapter 2 further shows us the power of the cross and trumps "God is no longer in the Ark." We all now have access to the Holy of Holies and can worship the Father freely without projecting an assigned location for such worship. As an evidence to this fact, He came down upon the disciples as cloven tongues of fire. With the outpouring of the Spirit came the ability for everyone to step into that position called righteousness.

When the Holy Spirit comes upon you, your story changes. The apostle Peter denied Jesus three times, but he was the very one who, after the Holy Ghost came upon him, stood up and declared very boldly:

For these are not drunken, as ye suppose, seeing it is but the third hour of the day. But this is that which was spoken by the prophet Joel. **Acts 2:15-16**

As a result, three thousand Jews were added to the church (see verse 41). Peter, who had been very timid, was the one who declared the gospel to the multitudes that day. Among other things, he preached:

Then judgment shall dwell in the wilderness, and righteousness remain in the fruitful field. **Isaiah 32:16**

The Holy Spirit Filling Unholy Men

When the Spirit comes, many get caught up in the mystery and try to figure out how the Holy Spirit can live in unholy people. One thing is clear: it is not because of our holiness, but because of God's righteousness by grace that we have access to such manifestations of God's Spirit. Romans 11:29 says: *"For the gifts and calling of God are without repentance."* These gifts are "without repentance," so we have no cause to brag. The giftings and callings are *a* work of grace and grace alone. God will never try to take righteousness from you. His intentions are for that righteousness to remain with you; that is your new nature.

Being Able to Distribute

"To profit" doesn't mean that you only experience sprinkles or only have just enough. Rather, it speaks of being able to distribute to others. Our covenant is not with a stingy God, and neither is it with an insufficient God. He is the God of more than enough and by His grace, He is calling us into a similar place of abundance and distribution. God knows how to put His wealth where His mouth is; therefore, He is disposed to judge sickness, poverty, and other needs that plague the human race. As in the feeding of the multitudes in Jesus' ministry on Earth, God is committed to sending us home, Word full, miracle full, and provision full. In like manner, you and I are called into a place of abundance so that we can be the type of servants of God who not only say, "the Bible says," but also act and cater to the needs of the saints by the distribution of our substance. As the Word of God declares:

"Then judgment shall dwell in the wilderness."

I just love the fact that judgment will dwell in the wilderness. When you decide to walk by faith, trusting the Lord all the way, God honors your faith. This becomes a type of covenant between you and Him. At this point, God is committed to settling disputes, stepping in when there is a challenge, releasing judgment in the wilderness, causing your enemies to be at peace with you, and much more. God honors every faith-inspired action by stepping in all the way because His integrity is on the line. Don't worry about enemies; God is after them. How do I know this? Because God said He would in His Word:

So shall they fear the name of the Lord from the west, and his glory from the rising of the sun. When the enemy shall come in like a flood, the Spirit of the Lord shall lift up a standard against him. **Isaiah 59:19**

The Lord shall cause thine enemies that rise up against thee to be smitten before thy face: they shall come out against thee one way, and flee before thee seven ways. **Deuteronomy 28:7**

That is our position and our blessedness in God.

"The Work of Righteousness"

Isaiah continued:

And the work of righteousness shall be peace; and the effect of righteousness quietness and assurance for ever. **Isaiah 32:17**

The work of righteousness shall be peace, wholeness, shalom, nothing missing, nothing broken. As a result of His righteousness, God wants to give you and me a mind of peace, quietness, and assurance forever.

God has not given us the spirit of fear; but of power, and of love, and of a sound mind. **2 Timothy 1:7**

The state of peace (tranquility in the presence or absence of chaos), assurance (a sense that all shall be well), and righteousness (being and knowing that you are on the same page with God) are the three components that make up the condition called "the mind of grace." When an individual possesses the mind of grace, regardless of what comes their way, they will not be knocked off their feet or forced into a state of being troubled or concerned. When the disciples of Jesus found themselves in trouble and were afraid of the wind, and whatever else they thought might be coming, the Bible records that Jesus was sleeping on a pillow (see Mark 4:38), resting in the midst of the storm. This confirms to us that we need not worry about anything that might befall us, because we now dwell in an entirely different realm—the realm of peace, quietness, and assurance forever. We are living in something like a bubble, and everything that comes at us from the left and the right just bounces off. This is why in the midst of a crisis, those around you are shocked to see that you are smiling. In the words of one of my sympathizers at a low point of my life, "You don't know what you are actually going through yourself." That is right, you are able to smile because you are part of a covenant that protects you from having a ruined life and, instead, gives you peace.

Jesus' Last Words

Many around the world would go an extra mile in honor of the last words of a dying person. In some cultures, such last words can become the rudder that changes the cause of men's lives for generations. When Jesus was leaving His disciples after the resurrection, He released declarations of peace. He understood that the greatest blessing to have in a time of chaos is the presence of tranquility. The final words of Jesus were reassuring words; words to live by which the current and future disciples could stand on in the face of life's challenges.

Peace I leave with you, my peace I give unto you: not as the world giveth, give I unto you. Let not your heart be troubled, neither let it be afraid. **John 14:27**

A perfect reflection of peace can be seen in the life of Jesus as He went about preaching the gospel. He went into the synagogue and started talking about the Spirit of the Lord being upon Him, and what the anointing the Father had placed upon Him would do. He said:

The Spirit of the Lord is upon me, because he hath anointed me to preach the gospel to the poor; he hath sent me to heal the brokenhearted, to preach deliverance to the captives, and recovering of sight to the blind, to set at liberty them that are bruised, to preach the acceptable year of the Lord. **Luke 4:18-19**

The people present that day were so offended by what Jesus was saying that they rose up and thrust Him out of the city, taking him to a high hill so that they could push Him off and kill Him (see verses 28-29). Fortunately for them, He passed through them and went His way. I don't know if they were frozen or if time stopped, but I just enjoy contemplating Jesus' peace on this occasion. As scriptures mention, Jesus did not die and they could not do anything to Him because it was not yet His time. I don't know about you, but I am determined that, by God's grace, I will not die before my time like many have. God will keep us, but we must learn to remain in the righteousness capsule that has been provided by grace; it is better than any bulletproof vest humans will ever create.

This promise is ours:

A thousand shall fall at thy side, and ten thousand at thy right hand; but it shall not come nigh thee. **Psalm 91:7**

For the purpose of understanding, consider a scenario in which you are in enemy territory. As you go about daily tasks, bullets are being fired, and there is no way of knowing if there is a safe zone. In such moments, you must step into the realm of the grace of God by recalling His promises to you. One thousand might be killed on your left, and ten thousand might be shot on your right, but for some reason, known as grace, those bullets will never touch you. Remembering His promises is your way out of harm and into grace—in this case, His protection. You might be in a tsunami or some other natural disaster, and everyone around you is dying, but you will live. It is not because you are any more special or immortal than the dying, but because you have decided to trust in the protective capsule of God, which is the grace dispensed to those who follow after His Word.

You might ask, "Is there really a scripture that speaks of or refers to such a capsule? Or is this just some cartoon illustration?" Try David's words in Psalm 91:

He that dwelleth in the secret place of the Most High shall abide under the shadow of the Almighty. I will say of the Lord, He is my refuge and my fortress: my God; in him will I trust. Surely he shall deliver thee from the snare of the fowler, and from the noisome pestilence. He shall cover thee with his feathers, and under his wings shalt thou trust: his truth shall be thy shield and buckler. **Psalm 91:1-4**

There is nothing that God cannot do, if we are willing to rest in Him. Listen now! The Lord isn't too weak to save you, and neither is His arm amputated. And He isn't getting deaf; neither are His ears stopped up. He can hear you when you call and touch you wherever you may be found in time and space. And yes, we came under the curse because of our sins, got cut off and also came short of His glory, BUT NOW, our lives are hidden with Christ in God. Now we belong to Christ Jesus, and though we once were far away from God, now we have been brought very near to Him because of what Jesus Christ has done for us with His blood. We are no longer aliens but we are the ones chosen by God, chosen for the high calling of priestly work, chosen to be a holy people, God's instruments to do his work and speak out for Him, to tell others of the night-and-day difference He made for us—from nothing to something, from rejected to accepted. Be at peace, child of God, for you are meant for more than ear has heard and more than eye has seen. Now let's get back to Isaiah 32:

And my people shall dwell in a peaceable habitation, and in sure dwellings, and in quiet resting places. **Isaiah 32:18**

I urge you not to accept anything in your life that isn't peace. The mind of grace is that state of being assured and knowing that although you are not up to a challenge, God Himself will complete you and bring you up to par by filling up all loopholes and/or discrepancies with grace.

And ye are complete in him, which is the head of all principality and power. **Colossians 2:10**

When Peter wrote to the early believers, he worded his letter this way:

Peter, an apostle of Jesus Christ, to the strangers scattered throughout Pontus, Galatia, Cappadocia, Asia, and Bithynia, elect according to the foreknowledge of God the Father, through sanctification of the Spirit, unto obedience and sprinkling of the blood of Jesus Christ: Grace unto you, and peace, be multiplied. **1 Peter 1:1-2**

What sort of language is Peter using here? Wasn't he a fisherman? Yes, he was, but he had come to the knowledge of having been chosen by God, despite all his idiosyncrasies and lack of formal education. You don't need to be a doctor, a lawyer, or a superschooled individual to serve God. The only requirement is having been with Jesus.

The Greatest of Jesus' Miracles

Have you noticed that among the greatest of Jesus' miracles were His words: *"Peace be multiplied"*? Peter wished that same blessing for the churches and their believers. He continued:

Blessed be the God and Father of our Lord Jesus Christ, which according to his abundant mercy hath begotten us again unto a lively hope by the resurrection of Jesus Christ from the dead, to an inheritance incorruptible, and undefiled, and that fadeth not away, reserved in heaven for you, who are kept by the power of God through faith unto salvation ready to be revealed in the last time. Wherein ye greatly rejoice, though now for a season, if need be, ye are in heaviness through manifold temptations: that the trial of your faith, being much more precious than of gold that perisheth, though it be tried with fire, might be found unto praise and honour and glory at the appearing of Jesus Christ: whom having not seen, ye love; in whom, though now ye see him not, yet believing, ye rejoice with joy unspeakable and full of glory: receiving the end of your faith, even the salvation of your souls. Of which salvation the prophets have enquired and searched diligently, who prophesied of the grace that should come unto you: searching what, or what manner of time the Spirit of Christ which was in them did signify, when it testified beforehand the sufferings of Christ, and the glory that should follow. **1 Peter 1:3-11**

Old Testament prophets searched for this grace but never understood it, and now we can enjoy it every single day. How wonderful is that?

Peter and Grace

Over and over again, Peter mentions this grace, enumerating the endless possibilities that are prepared for us through it. He highlights things we will solely get from favor and not from merit. In the second letter of Peter to the churches, he continues this teaching on grace, explaining:

Whereby are given unto us exceeding great and precious promises: that by these ye might be partakers of the divine nature, having escaped the corruption that is in the world through lust. And beside this, giving all diligence, add to your faith virtue; and to virtue knowledge; and to knowledge temperance; and to temperance patience; and to patience godliness; and to godliness brotherly kindness; and to brotherly kindness charity. For if these things be in you, and abound, they make you that ye shall neither be barren nor unfruitful in the knowledge of our Lord Jesus Christ. **2 Peter 1:4-8**

If these things abide in us, Peter concludes, we will be profitable. This is good news because not only do we now know that barrenness is not our portion, but we know how to get rid of it. It is of little or no consequence if there is famine in the land or not. God will cause ravens to feed you and me. In the midst of a drought, He will cause water to flow out of rocks for us; His supply is infinite! In the name of Jesus, we will not need to worry anymore. He finished the work, ceasing from His labors. So now everything that we need has been provided for, and we have been called to a life of peace. Praise God! As we close this chapter, can you shout it once again: *Grace! Grace!*

"Count your blessings. Once you realize how valuable you are and how much you have going for you, the smiles will return, the sun will break out, the music will play, and you will finally be able to move forward the life that God intended for you with grace, strength, courage, and confidence."

– Og Mandino

CHAPTER 3

Focusing on Grace

In this chapter, we will zoom in on the importance and benefits derived from focusing on grace. Concentrating on grace orients our thoughts and produces in us a grip and trust in God like nothing else. It is safe to say when we focus on grace, we constrain grace to locate us and bring about the miracles that display goodness, mercy, and favor. We tend to produce or bring about what we focus on most of the time. To be focused means to center one's interest and activities on something precise. Whatever that one thing is, it is the focal point, center of attraction, and the thing through which every other thing is filtered. Imagine for a minute what it means to make grace the center of everything you do; not only will that change how you do things, but it will also trigger what gets attracted to you. Focusing is therefore the shutting out of all else, bringing and maintaining in view the only thing that matters.

God is never idle, and everything He does is for a purpose. Focusing on grace causes, enables, and permits God to focus in return answers to our needs. We must believe that His faith is able—capable and productive—and for this reason, the Word of God says that in Him we live, move, and have our being (see Acts 17:28). When we are armed with this truth, nothing can turn us away from His path or throw us off guard. We must understand the extent to which our covenant with God covers us. The sacred Scriptures show us that He saves *"to the uttermost"* (Hebrews 7:25) and declares: *"If the Son, therefore, shall make you free, ye shall be free indeed"* (John 8:36). God goes way beyond our thinking, and that's why He will do *"exceedingly, abundantly above all that we can ask or think"* (Ephesians 3:20). You and I have some wild thoughts, and yet God can go and do above and beyond whatever we can think or ask.

Most of us have been asking less than we are supposed to. Asking beyond is necessary because we are asking from God, who is able to do exceedingly, abundantly above what we could ever think or ask. He can produce anything. That's the God we are serving, so start asking for much more. By the grace of God, I pray that He will open your eyes today and anoint you to understand what is yours.

The Presence of God's Spirit Changes Everything

At the beginning of Jesus' ministry, He entered the synagogue and read a chapter from the book of Isaiah that revealed an aspect of the grace of God and its workings. When He first opened the existing Scriptures in the synagogue, we are told that He said the following about the Spirit of the Lord:

Focusing on Grace

The Spirit of the Lord is upon me, because he hath anointed me to preach the gospel to the poor; he hath sent me to heal the brokenhearted, to preach deliverance to the captives, and recovering of sight to the blind, to set at liberty them that are bruised, to preach the acceptable year of the Lord. **Luke 4:18-19**

The purpose of the Spirit being upon us is to bring an enablement that will cause us to have answers (the gospel) for the brokenhearted. We must have Good News for the poor. We must be adequately enabled for those who have been held captive; we are the intermediaries for their liberation. The Spirit comes upon us and equips us with power from on high, so that we can bring recovery and restoration to those who have lost their sight and also to enable us to serve liberty to everyone who is bruised. Why was the Spirit of the Lord upon Jesus? It was so that He could give a suitable word to those in need (Colossians 4:6). He was anointed to bring such a word to every man or woman based on their circumstances.

We Are Not to Worry About What We Will Say

Worry is such a thief and has robbed many of several joyous moments which sadly may never be relived. When a person is overtaken by worry—the concern of what might be or not be—they become frozen, and regardless of what is before them, they are unable to step into the moment and grab the moment's blessings. Worry can hold you back from joy, expressing yourself in a relationship, releasing your full potential at work, or while carrying out your vision, it will handicap you from seeing possibilities even if they are presented in definite shades of black and white. For this reason, many are usually caught in the trap of concerning themselves with what they ought to say when challenged.

Our focus must be that we are graced or anointed to do what we have been called to do. If we are not anointed for the task at hand, the totality of our words will not bring about the recovery of sight. It will not heal the brokenhearted. It will not produce results of any kind. Therefore, I would much rather seek God for His grace—His anointing, His enablement—than solicit Him for specific words to speak. I would much rather be asking Him for His presence than seeking Him for His gifts. And I would certainly rather ask Him for His presence than strive for man's approval. I would rather seek God's presence than go after a pulpit; demand His presence than search for any opportunity to shine, whether in the pulpit or laying hands on those who are in need. This confusion has no substance and no eternal reward.

God must grace me. It is His grace that will cause my words to come across as words "seasoned with salt" and appropriate for the transformation of any situation. His grace can season my words, and when His grace seasons my words, those words will no longer come across as mere words. Instead, they become life-changing. Go on and study, fill your intellectual mind with as much information as you possibly can. Perfect yourself in whatever field you desire to fulfill your destiny through, but leave the flow of words and the momentous flow of destiny to grace. Let grace wear you like a man wears a glove. Permit yourself get into that realm in which after you speak, you wonder who was talking, as many have already experienced. There is a river that is waiting to flow out of you. It is the river of grace, carrying with it the words and actions for the moment. Always remember, grace knows the situation and has a better view than you. You have done your part and now, let grace do His. Let go and let God. The miracle hour is here. It is yours for the taking.

It is only when I am graced in this way that I can speak in like manner as Jesus, and declare that the words I release unto those I minister to *"are spirit and...life"* (John 6:63). It is then that I can know the difference between words that are *"spirit and life"* and words that the Bible says can actually kill (2 Corinthians 3:6). Let us desire more of God's presence so that we will never be guilty of killing people with our words. We will not destroy our communities and listeners, but rather produce life wherever we go. The grace of God upon us will make all the difference. Through the same grace of God that has abundantly blessed us, we will be able to bountifully minister life to others.

Only by God's Grace

As noted earlier in the book, the Word of God declares that if we believe on Christ, as the Scriptures have said, out of our bellies will flow *"rivers of living water"* (John 7:38). This can only be done by God's grace, and the totality of the gospel is summarized in the expression of that grace. Therefore, we understand that the grace of God is as perfect as the love of God, and that grace is refined by the love of God. For this reason, God has graced us to forgive, even as we have been forgiven. This is something new that we are walking in. It was the blood of Jesus that provided God the Father with grace to forgive. Before that blood was shed, the grace of God was limited in its exhibition or manifestation of mercy; as if God had no or limited patience, and evidently much anger or wrath revealed pestilence, disasters, and judgments of all sorts. Now, since that blood has been shed and the veil of the Temple has been torn, God has gone beyond all boundaries, and His love now extends much further. Thus, we serve a God who is all-knowing, and yet He accepts everyone and is willing to forgive everyone.

Mercy has triumph over judgment, and love is patient and kind. Love is not jealous, it does not brag, and it is not proud. Love is not rude, it is not selfish, and it cannot be made angry easily. Love does not remember wrongs done against it. Love is never happy when others experience evil, but it is always happy with the truth. Love never gives up on people because it never stops trusting, never loses hope, and never quits. Love has overcome anger.

Mercy and love are not suggesting that God now has a compromising stance toward sin but that the BLOOD that was shed on the cross provided a bill of satisfaction to every penalty levied for all offense. So, no, *"the Lord is not slack concerning his promise"* (2 Peter 3:9). Never!

The blood of Jesus has made it possible for us to enter a precious position of acceptance. The blood provided the propitiation for our sins, and not for ours only but also for the sins of the whole world. The blood of Jesus calmed down God's anger by being the full payment for sin and consequences for sin. God sent Christ Jesus to take the punishment for our sins and to end all God's anger against us. He used Christ's blood and our faith as the means of saving us from His wrath. In this way He was being entirely fair, even though He did not punish those who sinned in former times; for He was looking forward to the time when Christ would come and take away those sins. And now in these days also He can receive sinners in this same way because Jesus took away their sins. But isn't this unfair for God to let criminals go free, and say that they are innocent? No, for He does it on the basis of their trust in Jesus, who took away their sins. That's God's grace in action.

"Grace to Help in Time of Need"

Take a good look around and notice the countless undeserving people who are doing great things, enjoying wealth, walking in forgiveness, speaking from the pulpit, running companies, or coming up with big inventions. Many came from nothing to something. There is nothing meritorious really about their prominence. Follow the miracles, seek out the hand of grace, track it, and focus on the same in your life. The Word of God says that we should come before Him boldly that we may *"find grace to help in time of need"* (Hebrews 4:16). Whenever I'm in need, therefore, my search is not for a thunderous thing to occur, but for the grace of God to manifest. It is His grace that causes Him to extend His hand and causes me to be helped.

For us to understand such great grace, it is paramount for us to focus on certain aspects of it. Looking at grace from Jesus' viewpoint alone is not enough to understand it; we also need to look at it from the aspect of our own human frailties. The latter helps us see its impact on our day-to-day redemption, for we must work out our salvation with fear and trembling.

The Word of God declares:

We have this treasure in earthen vessels that the excellency of the power may be of God, and not of us. **2 Corinthians 4:7**

The question now is: How can God allow His Spirit to dwell in unholy people? How is it possible to produce such excellence from broken vessels? This is God's mission. And wouldn't you say it is working? Oh yes, it is working, and God is winning. No need going far in search for a testimony or case study; just look down your life and you will come to terms on why the angels sing so marvelously in celebration of God's salvation plan. You may think you are the only one who has been betrayed and stabbed in the back or wronged in more ways than one, but truth be told, no other person has been as betrayed, left alone, or abandoned as God Himself. How would you feel if you told someone you had created not to do something, and they did it anyway the minute you turned your back? That's what happened with God and His creation, and yet He forgives. How great is the grace of God! He was spat upon, beaten, sold for a few pennies, forgotten by those amongst whom He performed several miracles, yet while on the cross, He focused on grace and said, "Father, forgive them for they know not what they do."

This Grace Has "Appeared to All Men"

As we focus on grace and go through the Word of God, we will begin to see some very significant things. In Paul's letter to Titus, he writes:

For the grace of God that bringeth salvation hath appeared to all men, teaching us that, denying ungodliness and worldly lusts, we should live soberly, righteously, and godly, in this present world. **Titus 2:11-12**

The grace of God shows up for you and me, whether we are qualified for it or not. In fact, the only qualification for receiving the grace of God is that you are indeed a human being. By default, all humans are imperfect, weak, undeserving, and in need of assistance; therefore, no man or woman alive can complain that they have not been given what it takes. This grace has appeared *"to all men."* Do you remember the complaint of the impotent man by the pool of Bethesda? He said that every time the waters were troubled, there was no one to help him get in. But when Jesus came by the pool that day, the only question He entertained was: *"Wilt thou be made whole?"* (John 5:6). In other words, how badly do you want it? It is for all men everywhere, under every circumstance. The coming of Jesus disrupted the system and gave the impotent man a miracle without the angel showing up and stirring up the waters. Jesus, who is the symbol of grace, needs no time, premise, or law, for He Himself is the fulfillment of the law and the prophets. Since this grace has *"appeared to all men,"* no one can say they haven't had an opportunity. Neither can anyone say that it was somehow impossible for them, or that they were treated unfairly. The grace of God is available to whomever wants it.

He Is Faithful

The word *faithful* connotes the ability to deliver consistently over a period of time. It also presents the picture of someone who only comes in when their assignment is due as in the pickup guy is faithful or the sun is faithful in rising every day. In writing this, I immediately started laughing because that is what God is—faithful. He shows up when He is needed and seems dormant when all is well. Doesn't this just inspire peace? Regardless of human timing, He will deliver. You may not be seeing Him, you may not have goose bumps, hear His voice, or feel His touch, but just give it a few minutes and "The Faithful One" will show up. God's Word shows us that He who has promised is faithful (Hebrews 10:23; Hebrews 11:11). He is a Gentleman and does not push us to accept His ways, but He is faithful to present each one with the same opportunity.

For an additional piece to the "faithful" puzzle, kindly consider the delivery guy who is planning to show up at your doorstep one afternoon. Courier services have sent you mail to notify you of the arrival of your package. While the mail van is on its way, the driver has to deal with traffic conditions, weather conditions, and all sorts of conditions that bring about delay, yet they come and the delivery is carried out. What a mess every successful delivery goes through! Every time we are expectant, we need to understand that the moment we prayed, the answer was released. It may take time for the manifestation, but one thing is clear: regardless of the hoops to jump through and obstacles on the path of the delivery van, wait and keep on believing; your package shall be delivered right on time, for HE IS FAITHFUL WHO PROMISED.

Jeremiah has much to say about the thoughts of God. One of the most powerful passages in this regard is this:

For I know the thoughts that I think toward you, saith the Lord, thoughts of peace, and not of evil, to give you an expected end. **Jeremiah 29:11**

This does not speak of the end we expect, but of the end God Himself has destined for us. It is about time that we align ourselves with His expected end. The thoughts of the Lord will forever be higher than ours. To avoid inferior expectations and performance, we ought to know His mind and stay connected with His anticipation by design for us. When God looks at me and says that He has given me *"power to get wealth"* (Deuteronomy 8:18), I might be caught up at the same time wondering how I will pay my next month's house rent. He has graced me with enough to become wealthy, but I'm asking Him for just enough to get by for the day. God is faithful, and no amount of unbelief or circumstance will ever diminish the reality of His majesty and sovereignty.

A Double Standard?

A double standard describes a system that operates with two sets of rules within the same camp. In such cases, the rules allege to the existence of two classes or groups of persons; usually the superior class and the commoners. Certain scriptures cause some to wonder if there might exist a double standard with God in this regard. For example, 1 Corinthians 10:4 states: *"And did all drink the same spiritual drink: for they drank of that spiritual Rock that followed them: and that Rock was Christ."* The answer is: No, there is no double standard, and the Kingdom of God is not so. It is a perfect demonstration of a system with one set of rules provided to two classes of people. "As for me, my covenant is with you"—by implication, it is up to you for the taking. So what is going on here? The reason some seem to enter or access grace while others don't is just that most men choose far less for themselves than God has provided for them. Why not let Him choose for you? Then you will have the very best.

When God said, *"For sin shall not have dominion over you: for ye are not under the law, but under grace"* (Romans 6:14), we must understand the implication of the words *SHALL NOT.* This means that it cannot happen. Why? Because His grace has appeared to us. Grace, it would seem, is a soldier who fights for us. Grace is also a shield that guards us against harmful things. Grace paves the way before us and guards us as we walk that way. If we, therefore, walk on the paved way of grace, sin SHALL NOT dominate us.

The Difference between Evil and Judgment

The Word of God teaches that there is no temptation we will ever go through that those who have gone before us didn't encounter (1 Corinthians 10:13). Under normal circumstances, therefore, we ought not to be overtaken by a temptation. When a temptation comes to us, we should never say that it is God tempting us, because He is God, and He tempts no one with evil. There is nothing bad about God. He is all good. Therefore, we must learn the difference between the evil that attacks people and judgment that comes from God. These are two very different things.

What is judgment really? It is the reaction we receive to all our thoughts and actions. It is the constant reminder that as per Genesis 8:22, long as the Earth remains, seed time and harvest shall not cease. Please, my friend, understand this and come to terms with it sooner than later. Everything you do is a seed you plant, and the earth has a harvest it will give back to you in time. Do not be fooled;

whatever a man sows, that shall he also reap. Listen! God does not need to come and meddle with every little thing. There are laws set in the universe by Him already for checks and balances. God is busy doing good, and all the judgment you might be experiencing can easily be changed if you would just align your actions with the law.

God has allowed judgment to come as a servant of the law. The book of Romans tells us that soldiers serve the law (Romans 13:1-4). When a law is written, a soldier is expected to serve that law, and no one is above the law, not even you. In fact, you, too, are a servant to that law. However, thank God, His Word assures us that we are no longer under the Mosaic Law but under grace. (Allow me to add that grace is a much higher law.) However, grace did not come to abolish the law of seed time and harvest but to give the criminal a chance to seek something higher than himself.

A New Philosophy?

Is this then a new philosophy? No, not at all. The Word of God states that those of us who don't walk according to the flesh are now under the Spirit, and the Spirit we are under knows the law we now obey (Romans 8:4). Romans 8:2 tells us that this law is *"the law of the Spirit of life in Christ Jesus."* The other law was enmity with God. Those of us walking under this new law are no longer carnally minded, but rather spiritually minded. That's good news, isn't it?

Grace, however, does cause much controversy. Why? Let me give you an example. Paul wrote:

Shall we continue in sin, that grace may abound? **Romans 6:1**

His answer to this question was an emphatic: *"God forbid"* (Romans 6:2). Sin and grace cannot coexist. Would it be possible for us to bring hungry babies to men for breastfeeding? Of course not, because they have nothing with which to breastfeed a baby. In the same way, the law was inadequate in meeting our needs. The world, however, considers the wisdom of grace to be foolishness. Grace has appeared unto all men, with no set formulas. It is a manifestation of the goodness, mercy, and favor of the Lord. It is not designed to make any logical sense, but rather meant to be walked into and enjoyed.

When the Word of God asks us not to judge one another (Matthew 7:1), it is because you and I don't understand the grace that is keeping us, so we should stop analyzing the grace that is keeping some other person. It is no wonder, then, that Peter received the curt answer he got when he asked Jesus about another disciple. Jesus told him, "If it's my will for him to remain until I come back, how does that concern you? You must keep following me!" (John 21:20-22). Grace is God's business. Leave it to Him.

The Twelve?

How many disciples did Jesus have? Twelve, right? Then there were the seventy. But when all the seventy had left, who remained at His side? The twelve, right? When Jesus was having a meal in the Upper Room just before His arrest, how many disciples were with Him? Twelve, right? But remember Jesus' statement:

Have not I chosen you twelve, and one of you is a devil? **John 6:70**

When Jesus first called the twelve, He anointed them and sent them out to places He would later come (Luke 10:1). He empowered those twelve to teach and preach the gospel and to heal the sick, as He did. But, since one of them was a "devil," I ask you: How could the grace of God work in the one who was evil? The truth is that this grace of God functions in places you and I could hardly imagine. It goes into dark holes and pulls men and women out into the light. It finds them in their beer parlors and dance halls. It finds them in the midst of their addictions. God's grace will fish you out of wherever sin has pulled you. This is the craziness of His grace. This is where it doesn't make sense.

Am I saying that with all the sin that may have taken place in a person's life, God still wants to save them because of His grace? Yes, that's exactly what I'm saying, without which the death of Jesus on the cross was just mere formality. On the cross, that old rugged cross, was the price paid—completely paid, in full, for that matter. His salvation has appeared to all men, as Paul declared to Titus.

Grace Will Go with You

This grace that has appeared to all men wants to go with you to your office. It wants to touch your secret places. It wants to go where you wouldn't even want to mention. Hebrews 4:12 tells us that the Word of God is a *"discerner of the thoughts and intents of the heart"* and that it divides *"asunder [the] soul and spirit."* The grace of God enters where no one else could ever penetrate. There is no place on the face of the earth where it cannot be found. Even if I were in the mouth of a lion or the dungeon of some foreign palace, there is no place where grace could not find me and bring me relief. No wonder the Scriptures declare:

If the Son, therefore, shall make you free, ye shall be free indeed. **John 8:36**

How Jesus Faced the Death of His Friend Lazarus

We saw Jesus' declaration that day in the synagogue about the Spirit of the Lord being upon Him. Then He had to confront the death of His close friend Lazarus. Jesus went to the tomb of His dear friend and cried out, *"Lazarus, come forth"* (John 11:43), and Lazarus came back to life (verse 44). That's God's grace, the grace that makes all impossibilities suddenly possible. Am I saying that God can touch a murderer? Absolutely! That is exactly what grace is saying.

"The Word Is Nigh Thee"

Paul declared to the Romans:

The word is nigh [us], even in [our] mouth, and in [our] heart. **Romans 10:8**

That's why the more you increase in the knowledge of God, the more grace will manifest itself to you. When Jesus was asking His disciples how long He would be with them (Matthew 17:17), it was because He was the tangible symbol of grace. The Word of God says in John 1:16 that He has been given to us as *"grace for grace."* Christ is grace unto us. So when Jesus was asking them how long He would be with them, He was merely asking them when they would have a change of story. He needed to go away so that the grace of God could be made available for everyone.

God-Appointed Officers

As noted earlier, the Scriptures state that a policeman is a minister of God:

Let every soul be subject unto the higher powers. For there is no power but of God: the powers that be are ordained of God. Whosoever, therefore, resisteth the power, resisteth the ordinance of God: and they that resist shall receive to themselves damnation. For rulers are not a terror to good works, but to the evil. Wilt thou then not be afraid of the power? Do that which is good, and thou shalt have praise of the same: for he is the minister of God to thee for good. But if thou do that which is evil, be afraid; for he beareth not the sword in vain: for he is the minister of God, a revenger to execute wrath upon him that doeth evil. **Romans 13:1-4**

To throw more light on this fact, please consider the following scenario. A policeman was doing his regular office work one day when he felt like driving out. The only reason he could find for stepping out of the office was to place an early order for lunch as a surprise for his friends. He wanted to treat them to a meal as a team appreciation effort. Simultaneously, a robbery plan was in progress a few blocks away from the restaurant.

Almost as if these two events were designed with the same timelines in mind, the officer by sheer intuition decided that he should drive down another street. Right there before his eyes, looking at people's faces and their behavior led him to suspect foul play, and one thing leading to another brought about the robbers getting apprehended. Grace knows how to lead an officer, a teacher, or a doctor for lives to be saved and order maintained. Grace leads the pastor for the sermon that preserves and fosters destiny. It is all grace! In the case of the officer, the bandits were more than he could handle, but he made a call and reinforcement came to the scene sooner than might be expected because his colleagues were just around the corner. One act of grace saved people from gunshot wounds and the robbers were apprehended.

Doing the Unimaginable

When the Egyptians were pursuing the people of God, the Israelites were on foot, and the Egyptians were in their chariots. It seemed that God's people didn't have a chance. But God came on the scene and began popping the wheels off the Egyptian chariots (Exodus 14:25). The grace of God will do the unimaginable. When I sit and meditate on these things, it blows my mind. How great the grace of God is! It can do anything for you.

Grace Parted the Red Sea

Why did God part the Red Sea? The Scriptures record this event as a product of His grace: *"his mercy endureth for ever"* (Psalm 136:13). Why doesn't this psalm say that He parted the sea because He had such exceptional strength? Clearly, God isn't interested in showing up to show off or to impress anyone. He is God! He isn't interested in boasting before others as in someone who wants to prove a point about their identity. All that He does is the result of His mercy and grace; for the salvation of humanity and the furtherance of the Kingdom's agenda. His grace appeared, and the sea parted. Period! And the reason?

"For his mercy endureth forever."

The Bible tells us that the pillar of fire stopped the Egyptians in their tracks, stalling them in place until the Israelites could get across the sea (Exodus 14:24). As a matter of fact, the Israelites had not fully crossed yet when the enemy was released to follow. Their lead had been just enough enticement for the Egyptians. The fire seemed to be dying out, so the Egyptians continued their pursuit. God waited because He had already given the word, and that word was that these Egyptians the Israelites had seen they would see no more (Exodus 14:13). And now His grace was bringing that word to pass.

On several occasions, the children of Israel may have felt like they were going in circles, but a word had been released, and it would be fulfilled. I can just imagine how the last person in line crossing the sea must have felt. Would they be forced back to Egypt? It was the grace of God that prevented it that day. Let your mind and spirit be awakened to the grace of God for your situation.

Ordered Steps

If this grace could work in Judas, how much more for you? Don't be deceived by the enemy. You have a better covenant in Christ Jesus than was available to Judas. So if grace was available to him, it is even more so available to you today. The Word of God says that the steps of the righteous are *"ordered by the Lord"* (Psalm 37:23). How? By His grace. It is His grace that teaches you not to put your feet somewhere you might be harmed.

I'm sure that you probably had an experience in which you were about to step out or do something, but then it seemed as if your whole system just didn't agree with that move. What do you think that was? It was God's grace waking your consciousness to possible danger and/or giving you the opportunity to redirect your steps. This is what God's grace has done and will do for you and me.

Having Been with Jesus

When people heard Jesus' disciples speaking eloquently as they delivered the word of righteousness, they were surprised and marveled, knowing that they were men without much educational training. Their conclusion was *"that they had been with Jesus"* (Acts 4:13). When you are walking in the grace of God, you, too, will begin to do things people never expected you to do. Any man or woman who clings to the Word of God as their only source of life will not only survive but thrive in the desert. They can survive anywhere in this world because the grace of God will work on their behalf.

Strength in Weakness

When we look into the word *strength*, immediately we identify a word that we can apply or use on multiple platforms, such as the strength of an engine, the strength of an athlete, or even the strength of a storm. But in this book, we are referring to strength as the ability, power, or authority that primarily operates in the realm of the invisible, and has results showing in the physical realm, in the natural, and we can talk about horsepower referring to the engine power of a car. In the case of Jesus calming the storm or any other miracle He performed for that matter, we see a man who releases words to circumstances, animate and inanimate things, and we see those things beginning to take form in obeisance to the words. Storms calmed down without any natural weapons used; the sick were healed without any medication; a fish carried within it the coin needed to pay taxes; and the dead were brought back to life, just to mention a few. No wonder His disciples said, "What manner of man is this, who has authority even with the winds?"

This conversation will sound foreign to anyone who is ignorant of the different realms on which we live. As humans, we live in three realms and relate with them all with the aid of certain communication tools. These levels consist of the spiritual realm, intellectual realm, and the physical realm, respectively. All forms of creation—things that come into being in the physical realm— all proceed forth from the spiritual realm, which is the strongest of all three.

Nothing happens in the visible realm without first happening in the invisible realm. God is not looking for supermen; this is all "muscle strength," but He is looking for "closet strength." In its purest and unadulterated form, the strength of God within an individual is cultivated upon the mountains of seclusion and intent while sharpened by the valor of vision bathed in love. Anyone who has strength with God also has strength with men. As Paul very well puts it, "the weapons of our warfare are not carnal but mighty through God to the pulling down of stronghold..."

This strength is only sought by the weak and displayed by the meek, for the meek shall inherit the earth. The Book of Acts tells of Simon, who wanted to buy the power of God with money. When Simon saw that the Holy Spirit was given when the apostles placed their hands upon people's heads, he offered money to buy this power. "Let me have this power too," he exclaimed, "so that when I lay my hands on people, they will receive the Holy Spirit!" But Peter replied, "Your money perishes with you for thinking God's gift can be bought! You can have no part in this, for your heart is not right before God. Turn from this great wickedness and pray. Perhaps God will yet forgive your evil thoughts. The strength of God is not for sale, and neither is it for display or self-gain." In the words of John Dalberg-Acton, "Power tends to corrupt, and absolute power corrupts absolutely." So, such strength requires maturity, purity of intentions, self-control, and the father of all promises—patience.

God is looking for people who will acknowledge that they are weak (meaning open and in need) so He can pour into them strength for weakness. We must understand that the power or grace of God *"is made perfect in weakness"* (2 Corinthians 12:9). So, if you keep acknowledging your weakness by always desiring God to fill up your shortcomings, you will find His grace taking you places you have never been before.

God isn't saying that we should marry our weaknesses. He is only asking us to acknowledge them, recognize them as part of humanity, and become acquainted with the need to call for divinity, knowing deep within that we are made for covenant! As we engage in such practice, we open up to Him so that His grace can function and enable us to overcome all sorts of challenges. The Word of God demands us to take heed when we think we stand because that's when we can fall (1 Corinthians 10:12). We need to stop all boasting and let God be God. The power behind all achievement does not lie in your strength but rather in His ability. The fact that you have been paying your bills is because He is wealthy and generous and has channeled some over to you. Other seemingly better-placed people than you and me are lying in the gutter, as drunk as can be. You and I are not in similar situations only because of God's grace.

How God's Grace Functioned in Judas

I have racked my brain trying to understand how God's grace worked in Judas. He was a very crooked man, and whatever he did, he focused solely on himself. He was the type of person who would fellowship with opposing sides and feel at home with both. One of the ways we know that people gave good offerings to Jesus' ministry is the fact that Judas stole so much from the treasury, and yet many didn't even notice. Then, when Judas and the other disciples were sent out by Jesus, they all returned giving the same report; demons fled before them. Amazingly, God worked through Judas, despite his stealing ways. For more than three years, Judas mingled with grace, dined with grace, and was shielded by grace. Clearly, grace played its role as grace, but Judas failed to settle on the most advantageous option—the change grace offered; rather, he permitted the devil to enter him and drag him into the grave.

Please carefully consider the following attributes of grace to help comprehend this section. This conversation crafted around the life of Judas is intended for you not to quickly dismiss yourself from the picture, because in more ways than one, Judas is the symbol of the child of God who walks and talks with God, yet misses one or more God attributes, thus betraying the master on a daily basis. Please quit thinking of yourself more highly than you ought. There is but one God: He alone is Holy, flawless, and ALL GOOD, and all else are yet to be like HIM. If you grasp the three points below, you will be a better recipient of the grace of God.

1. Grace does not operate on a conditional basis: It is not affected or influenced by location or environment. It is not subject to race or age; neither is it a servant to gender. Hence, equal treatment for all.

2. Grace does not operate from the standpoint of foreknowledge or precognition; it does not manifest in an individual because it knows something about their past, present, and/or future. Consequently, grace shows no favoritism because of social status.

3. Grace is assignment-oriented, or function-focused. It is a system and does not pick and choose who to go to and who to avoid. It does not operate as in two-way traffic: It fits into no one's mold, but everyone can access its mold. Grace will stand with you from the moment of your conception until the time you leave Earth. As a result, grace cannot be bribed or cajoled into doing something other than its intended use; its hand cannot be forced into doing anything, whatsoever, but that which it is designed to do.

As you can see, grace acts independently of everything else that is human, yet manifests to all men toward one goal—salvation. As a result, you must strongly consider that the manifestation of spiritual gifts is not the guarantee of your salvation, for *"the gifts and callings of God are without repentance"* (Romans 11:29). In fact, the manifestation of supernatural abilities is a work of grace. It is God saying, "Hopefully my goodness draws this one in on my presence today." The fact that God has given you all of the giftings you have isn't a visa for Heaven. You will still have to go through Jesus because He is the only way, and not through any gifts.

This is why in the last days, many will come with *"great signs and wonders"* and deceive many—even *"the very elect"* (Matthew 24:24). Don't be surprised when someone is on fire for God one day, and the next, you have to wonder about them. They say they're fine, but you sense that they're not. They might very well have fallen from grace.

It is possible to have great grace upon your life and still fall from it, not making it through to the fulfillment of God's assignment for your life. If you received a prophetic word or divine insight from someone, a dream or a vision doesn't guarantee that such information will materialize or come to pass automatically or even that you will make it through, especially if you are not really interested in holding on. All promises in scripture depend on conditions that we have to fulfill as our own part of the bargain to such words of prophecy.

We have been called into a COVENANT SYSTEM. God has a part, and we have a part as well. It is through the combination of these two that we experience grace and finality. If you hold on to what you have been given, then yes, you will make it to the end. If you don't, you can't blame anyone else because this grace has *"appeared to all men."* You have your chance.

Know that you have been empowered and are being enabled daily, and if you are making it, despite the obstacles, it is because of God's grace. Only His grace can take us through the attacks and oppositions of the enemy. When you walk in the light of God and your goggles are the goggles of grace; when you see huge things emerging to confront you, you will not feel dead or feel like a grasshopper. You will feel like a giant because you are looking at things through the eyes of grace. God's Word in our hearts brings that grace to us. Shout it now: *Grace! Grace!*

"The bridge of grace will bear your weight, brother. Thousands of big sinners have gone across that bridge, yea, tens of thousands have gone over it. Some have been the chief of sinners and some have come at the very last of their days but the arch has never yielded beneath their weight. I will go with them trusting to the same support. It will bear me over as it has for them."

– Charles Spurgeon

CHAPTER 4

The Eyes of Grace

But Noah found grace in the eyes of the Lord. **Genesis 6:8**

In this section of our study, we shall be digging into what it means to have the eyes of grace, look at someone with the eyes of grace, or have someone look at you with the eyes of grace. To master this, we shall go back and consider the definitions. Firstly, let us start with the scripture in Genesis 6:8 as mentioned above. Noah found grace in the eyes of God. This is saying that when God looked down at Noah, He looked at him with eyes that have been influenced by grace. "In the eyes of" the Lord—an opinion of grace had been formed, and everything the Lord would do from that time onward would be based on His grace view of Noah. In Chapter 3, we mentioned three things that everyone needs to understand when dealing with grace. If we bring those three components into this picture, this is what we will see: Since grace is not controlled by any human and does not conform to any human's mold but is rather open for humans to fit into its mold, then it is safe to say there is something in Noah's mannerisms that caught the eyes of grace. As in a lock and key, Noah, being the key, fitted into the hole called grace and they both clicked. Now, let us exit the expression "in the eyes of" and talk about the word *grace*.

God's Grace

The grace of God is more than just a woman's name. It does not speak of natural favor or ability. The application of the grace of God is not as you probably have heard it used in statements like: "He walks with so much grace." This use of *grace* denotes a certain amount of class, beauty, or distinction. As Dictionary.com relates it, *grace* is "elegance or beauty of form, manner, motion, or action." *Grace* can also refer to "a pleasing or attractive quality or endowment." *Grace* is also "a manifestation of favor, especially by a superior." The grace of God is none of these, and it does not refer to prayers before a meal either.

God's grace is something apart from all these human uses of the word. His grace is the manifestation of His goodness, mercy, and favor. Looking at various scripture verses that mention grace enables us to see it in the fullness of its meaning. Let's begin here with Genesis, where we find the first mention of this term *grace*: In God's dealings with humanity, two dispensations classify the Bible, and they are law and grace. The Bible also has two Testaments, namely Old and New Testaments or Old and New Will. The law is prescribed and enforced in the Old Testament in this way: "the soul that sinneth shall die," while grace is birthed in the New Testament declaring "mercy triumphs over judgment—freed from the curse of the Law" with the death of the Savior, Jesus Christ, on the cross. This transition from law to grace is the foundation for all biblical interpretation.

Noah Found Grace

But Noah found grace in the eyes of the Lord. **Genesis 6:8**

It is somewhat odd that Noah, a character in the Old Testament, would find grace. This was a little different because, in a general sense, grace was not an Old Testament concept or practice. The only explanation for this to have happened is if he stepped into a realm way ahead of his time. Noah is mentioned to have specifically found grace because everyone else in his time was going their own way and doing whatever was pleasing to them. Settling on either the good or the bad route on the side of grace is the singular thing that separates those who conform to grace and those who do not. Grace has not just appeared to all men and provided equal opportunity for salvation, but it is also the yardstick or standard by which each of us benefits from this opportunity.

So grace not only teaches us to say NO! to ungodliness but also sets the time and date for that decision. The tendency for all humans is to push this appointed time into the distant future, primarily because we do not understand the evil in sin, BUT grace always demands of us to settle on transformational actions NOW. When Moses confronted the children of Israel because some had turned against God, he asked for those who were on the Lord's side to come and stand with him. This command brought sudden judgment in that the ground opened up and swallowed those who still stood on the opposing side (Numbers 16). The children of Israel were forced to decide at that instant, and there was no time to go home and sleep on it. "TODAY is the day and NOW is the time of salvation," says grace. By the way, that opening of the ground and swallowing people is what falling short of the expectations and standards of the law looks like—instant judgment.

When men found grace in the sight of God in these isolated incidents of Old Testament times, they felt blessed. They had been favored apart from all others (for example, Exodus 34:9 and Esther 5:8). Today, however, we are living in the age of grace in which grace is available for everyone. Grace and the works of grace are all around us, and we can avail ourselves of their favor.

Jacob Found Grace

The experience of Noah we just talked about brought out what it means to have found grace in the eyes of the Lord, and now we shall be talking about finding grace in the eyes of another human. In this case, we shall use the story of Jacob and his brother Esau, and as scripture puts it, Jacob found grace in his brother's eyes:

And Jacob went on his way, and the angels of God met him. And when Jacob saw them, he said, This is God's host: and he called the name of that place Mahanaim. And Jacob sent messengers before him to Esau, his brother unto the land of Seir, the country of Edom. And he commanded them, saying, Thus shall ye speak unto my lord Esau; Thy servant Jacob saith thus, I have sojourned with Laban, and stayed there until now: and I have oxen, and asses, flocks, and menservants, and womenservants: and I have sent to tell my lord, that I may find grace in thy sight. **Genesis 32:1-5**

This scripture reveals the portion of the story between these two brothers: Jacob and Esau. As brothers growing under the same roof, they had a relatively good life, with some issues arising here and there, as is the case with many siblings. There was nothing at the time that they could not traverse and put behind them, especially in the case in which Jacob used his brother's hunger and desire for immediate food gratification to trade birthright positions with him. Things seemed manageable until Jacob went the extra mile to steal his brother's blessings; he had crossed the line this time. Temperaments were fuming, and the flames of fury gushed out of Esau, and it became a matter of life and death. "Jacob must die" became the interpretation of the emotions that filled the atmosphere and more like the last words that carved out Jacob's memories of his brother. With the aid of his mother, Jacob went into hiding at an uncle's house miles away from his once loving and familiar environment.

After more than twenty years in hiding and unresolved tension between them, a promise from the Lord prompted Jacob to head back home. But this awakened fear for the unknown reaction of his brother towards him when they eventually met. En route to meeting his brother, Jacob sent a peace offering of animals, servants, children, and even wives ahead of him, hoping that his brother would forgive the treachery done to him years prior. (Please, read more on the struggle over the birthright in Genesis, chapters 25 and 27). Now, years had passed, and Jacob was hoping to find grace (in this case, grace means forgiveness or mercy) in his brother's eyes. And he did.

If a man's ways please grace, grace will cause even his enemies to be at peace with him. Jacob had wrestled all night with the Lord and broke forth into a place of blessing. His life was changed from the one who "needed to cheat to make it" to the one who is called "prince with God." When you wrestle with the Lord in prayer and making things right with Him, you shall find grace in the eyes of men.

People in a relationship (husband and wife, kids and parents, friends, coworkers, etc.) often do things to please each other so that they might find grace in each other's eyes. This type of grace talks about favors and just a sense of cordiality. The grace of God does not function in that manner; there is nothing you can do to earn, as in a reward, the grace of God. Notwithstanding, your actions and disposition will position you to better access and appropriate the grace that has appeared unto you.

Offerings and Grace

Whenever you hear the word *offering*, I am sure like many others your mind goes to the contributions brought in on worship/prayer service days that go into a basket or collection plate. Offerings are beyond this: An offering is anything dispensed as a gift to someone, such as a birthday present; anything given for the enjoyment of someone, as in food, drink, or clothes; or anything administered in honor for someone. Such things could go from services, money, to material things. As a general rule, whenever you think or hear the word *offering*, think exchange, bargain, return, give-and-take, swap or trade.

The Eyes of Grace

Nothing you do in this world goes unnoticed. In the Book of Genesis, the eighth chapter and twenty-second verse, we are told that as long as the earth continues to exist, there will be planting of seeds and a corresponding harvest from those seeds. Cold and hot, summer and winter, day and night will not stop. So how does this all play out with grace? This may be the most challenging question you will ever ask and, if I might add, the most life-changing revelation you might ever walk into. So let us bring it all together.

Firstly, Genesis 8:22 is a LAW, and it cannot be broken; it is the law of sowing and reaping, which makes sure that everyone is rewarded for the things they have done, be they of evil origin or good origin. This way, there is a system of check and balances, and God does not need to punish or reward anyone. Each individual creates the reward they hope to wrap around their life. This law keeps the world moving in the right direction and everyone getting in this lifetime what is due them from the seeds they sowed. For the law breaker or the one who sows evil seeds, this could certainly turn out to be a nightmare, because evil-pressed down, shaken together, rolling over harvest is not fun as depicted by the African proverb: "Ninety-nine days for the thief and one day for the owner." BUT the good obviously is a thing of celebration.

Secondly, grace is also a law that seeks the law-abiding and law-breaking citizen, calling them both to a place of not just help in the face of a challenge, but also a place of empowerment to go through it. Grace is only as relevant as there are humans for where sin abounds, grace much more.

Grace and the law of seed time and harvest time work hand in hand. Regardless of the projected harvest as indicated by Genesis 8:22, we can call on grace and be carried into the undeserving realm.

With this in mind, each offering—be it in cash, in-kind, or in actions of service—a reward of access is compounded to yield unto the donor grace-ability dividends. One scriptural example is Cornelius (Acts 10:1-8 and 22-48). In Old Testament times, a woman named Shechem vowed to give according to the grace she encountered (Genesis 34:11).

Joseph Found Grace

In another Old Testament case, Joseph found grace in the eyes of his owner, because of his faithful service, and was made overseer of all that he had (Genesis 39:4).

Saving Grace

The most famous form of grace found in the Bible is known as *saving grace*. In a general sense, this is a New Testament term, but it was also experienced at times (by faith) by men of old. When Abraham was interceding concerning the wicked cities of Sodom and Gomorrah (Genesis 18:16-33), he was calling on the saving grace of God.

What is saving grace? Saving grace is manifested when God comes in and pulls you out of a mess you don't deserve to be rescued from. As believers in Christ, we all know that we were sinners and that we should be suffering the wages of our sin especially by death, but God came and saved us by His grace. That is His saving grace. It brings healing where there is no medication, forgives the worst of criminals and turns him into a preacher, reveals wealth where there are no resources, picks up prisoners and turns them into kings, and takes a barren woman and turns her into a mother of seven. Oh, grace, what a wonder You are! You transform and save to the utmost.

The love of God that produces saving grace is found in the heart of every creature because God said that He would write His laws on our hearts (Jeremiah 31:33). It is God's saving grace within each of us that causes us to pray prayers like: "Oh God, if You are real, show up." Something inside of you told you to pray that kind of prayer. Despite the fact that such a prayer comes across as being very simple (especially to those who pray long and seemingly thunderous prayers), it is real because it relies on God's saving grace. Don't misunderstand me. The point here is not if God answers prayers because of their length, but He answers when we depend upon His saving grace and pray in agreement with His will, be it written in scripture or revealed.

In the course of Jesus' ministry, Peter, one of His disciples, experienced very special moments with his master. On one of these occasions, Jesus had released the disciples with instructions—go on ahead and I will meet you on the other side. It is reported that while they were at sea, they encountered a scary storm that sent their hearts pounding as they wondered what the next couple of minutes held for them. Amidst this drama came Jesus walking on water as if to twist the knife in the wound; this strange sight prompted the disciples to feel even worse, crying out in fear.

To calm these grown men who probably were grabbing each other for support in this menacing moment, Jesus said, "Fear not, it is I." Oh, how reassuring to hear such words. Peter at this time not only took those words seriously but responded by saying, "Lord if it is You, bid me." And Jesus said, "Come." With courage, Peter stepped out in faith and walked towards Jesus. This heroic moment soon came to a halt when Peter observed the boisterous wind and began to sink. Focusing on the wind rather than the voice of the Master ushered in a moment of weakness, and Peter was trailed down the depth of the dark, monstrous sea. "Help! Help! I am sinking" were the words that accompanied the outstretched arm seeking rescue.

Peter had not only lost faith and was now unbelieving, but he had also sold out the authenticity of the Master's voice for the tempestuous winds. This great sin, as stipulated in the book of John, qualified him with the reward of condemnation as it is written, "Whoever believes *and* has decided to trust in Him [as personal Savior and Lord] is not judged [for this one, there is no judgment, no rejection, no condemnation]; but the one who does not believe [and has decided to reject Him as personal Savior and Lord] is judged already [that one has been convicted and sentenced], because he has not believed *and* trusted in the name of the [One and] only begotten Son of God [the One who is truly unique, the only One of His kind, the One who alone can save him]."

This terrible trade cost him stability over the waters and bought for him a downward trail to the abyss; BUT for grace. Peter failed the merit test, and that qualified him for a walk with grace! That is the saving grace we are talking about—not rendering every man his wages according to the sin committed but rather reaching out and saving the LOST out of the path of physical and/or eternal death. As described by Jesus in these words in Mark 2:17: "Those who are healthy have no need of a physician, but [only] those who are sick; I did not come to call the righteous, but sinners [who recognize their sin and humbly seek forgiveness]."

When Abraham prayed concerning Sodom, did God tell him that He would take care of Lot? I don't think so. And yet the Bible says that God remembered Abraham and saved Lot (Genesis 19:29). We have a lot to learn about effective prayer. We must approach the throne of grace similarly to the children of a loving Father who is faster, wiser, and stronger than all else, and we must call on His saving grace. Very often, we forget that we are still His children. This forgetfulness turns us into "adults of God," taking control and wanting to do things by ourselves, rather than children of God who depend on their Father's ability to save them. Suddenly we want to act as if we are on the same level as God. We will forever be His children while He will forever be Father God: faster, wiser, and stronger than all of us put together. Stop considering yourself to have arrived; call out to your Heavenly Father, for He is the graceful Savior, and there is room for more and greater.

Noah Was Saved

We know that Noah built an ark by faith (Hebrews 11:7). Constructing an ark at the time to secure shelter from rain did not make sense because rain had never fallen on the earth. Noah definitely heard from God, and when he heard from God, he believed that God was trying to save him. This unveils a major lesson for us on how to walk in the grace of God. The Father—who sees more than we do, hears more than we do, and is all-knowing—gives us direction with the intention of saving us. Obedience is a major key to walking and procuring the benefits of saving grace.

So, what did Noah do? He embraced the saving grace of God. Very few of God's children who receive warnings from the Holy Spirit consider that God is trying to save them. Instead, most of us believe that He is about to let judgment fire fall on us.

The psalmist David declared:

O give thanks unto the Lord; for he is good: because his mercy endureth for ever. **Psalm 118:1**

In this scripture lies the basis of our prayers; we pray expecting because He is good and not because of our own goodness.

Don't Be Deceived

The greatest weapon the enemy can have over the child of God is the weapon of ignorance. If someone is without knowledge, regardless of their military strength they are up to no good in the face of combat. All knowledge is only as relevant as its application. Therefore, knowledge is only as important as its intended use. So, in your getting, you must get understanding. A person without understanding is walking a very slippery slope and knows not when he will be taken down. A king without understanding rules the city whose high walls contain no gates. Beware then, lest any man spoil you through philosophy and vain deceit, after the tradition of men, after the rudiments of the world, and not after Christ; for to be deceived is to be taken off course and set on a path of destruction. The devil is the master deceiver, and he will do his best to keep you away from the truth; grace is your way out, for by strength shall no man prevail.

Remember that grace equals goodness, mercy, and favor. When the Bible mentions mercy, it is speaking of God's grace. What is mercy? Mercy is pardon or letting go of someone's offense. You and I must be conscious of God's mercy. As His Word declares: His mercy is *"new every morning"* (Lamentations 3:23). In Him, we live, move, and have our being. As it is with the sun that faithfully rises every day, so is the renewal of His mercy and goodness. The miracles we experience are all by grace lest any man should boast. Give God the glory for all He has done and all that He will continue to do. Don't let the devil deceive you into thinking that your prayers are the reason why God is God; many have gotten to a place of pride in which they think their "gigantic prayers" are the reason for all the big things we see. Such high-mindedness is the reason for great corruption, and such pride precedes a fall (Proverbs 16:18). When you base your prayer life on yourself, rather than on the cross, you can't expect God to respond. Many people are praying to themselves, and God doesn't even hear them.

Let your faith rest not on how many days you have fasted, but on the God who answers prayer when you call on Him. Get out of yourself and into His grace, and miracles will happen.

Get Excited

Some time ago, we had the privilege of attending the meetings of a visiting minister who was the main speaker at an evangelistic campaign. I witnessed unique manifestations of the move of God with this minister. In the course of his ministration, he declared, "There will be three hundred miracles here today," and that got me excited and bewildered at the same time. In fact, I wondered within me: was he just guessing, suggesting, or proclaiming? He said it often, with such certainty. He could have said two hundred and fifty or five hundred, but he said three hundred. After a time of preaching and teaching from the Holy Scriptures, he started praying for people by calling out different conditions. At this point, I got even more perplexed. He would say, "There are ten people here with such and such," and at that declaration, the power of God would come upon certain ones and he would begin counting. "One, two, three, four…" then nine and ten. I could hardly believe my eyes and ears. I had not yet seen things happen in this fashion. "This can only be God," I muttered to myself. "How else can this be?" I continued debating within. BUT, yes, that is it! Only God could have told him; this was so precise, and he did not need to "push" anyone. He spoke from the stage while the demonstration of the spirit happened with the crowd. God was flowing with a human being in an amazing harmony. When we flow with God's amazing grace, marvelous things happen. We can hear Him speak and we declare what He said, knowing that it will come to pass just as He said it. That experience forever changed my life.

Please decide NOW, never to settle for anything less than God's best for your life, and settle NOW that you will seek and pursue

God's best for you with every fiber of your being. No other alternatives! We solely must flow with His grace, for He is Lord—not you and not I. He could take us out in less than a second. There are, in fact, times when He does not hear our prayers (Psalm 66:18). Too often we pray in pride. We declare our past victories in an attempt to push God toward answering. Yes, God pops people out of wheelchairs, but we must never forget that it's not by might or power, but by the Spirit of the Lord. It is not our strength that works a miracle, but a mighty God working in and through us.

Be Careful to Have Pure Motives

By the grace of God, I have been able to witness the move of God in diverse ways. Just as the scriptures declare, "these signs shall follow them that believe." It is the norm to expect miracles, for the Lord promised to be with us confirming the Word with signs following. Blind eyes opening, ears being unstopped, and people being liberated from wheelchairs are nothing short of the norm in the kingdom. Care must be taken to give God all the glory. This might seem tricky because there is no measuring rod with which to evaluate our complete disposal to God, of the glory directed towards us. We must then use the tool of examining motives whenever we testify, publish on the World Wide Web, or just freely talk about a miracle. These questions will help you better communicate:

Why am I narrating this story?

What do I need to prove?

Why this person?

Why the Internet?

Why this time?

From this, you will know or be able to discern if it is to publicize who God is or who we are or your ministry. He deserves all the glory; we don't. And if we make the mistake of advertising ourselves, God can shut us down so fast it will make our heads spin. When we do something like that, we start a war with Him (Isaiah 42:8). If we lift Him up in our music, in our day-to-day relationships, and in all that we do, He will explode over us with His saving grace.

Don't Try to Walk in Someone Else's Grace

This section, in the discussion on the topic of grace, is a pivotal aspect of this teaching. Up till now, we have been mostly talking about the grace for salvation that has appeared unto all men as revealed in the book of Titus, second chapter and the eleventh verse. But at this point, we shall go even deeper and mention a particular level of grace that operates on people because of their divine destiny or the divine reason for their existence.

There is such a thing as purpose—our reason for being. Our purpose is the definite action we are to carry out in the course of our existence. You and I are a verb in motion. You are, therefore, either teaching and so a teacher, helping and so a helper, coaching so a coach, treating and so a physician, nurse or pharmacist, and the list goes on and on.

The Eyes of Grace

Have you ever considered that the world we live in and life in general would be a "valley of boredom" if everyone was meant to do the same thing, say the same thing in a similar manner, and walk the same path? Coming to this world would be so purposeless that dying would be a mere formality. In such a world, there would never be a conversation centered on inheritance or legacy, and we would just be walking robots. But, as many as are the climatic conditions, so are there differences in vegetation, topography, races, belief systems, etc. Every environment, family, culture, and belief system has its fingerprints on every individual. There is so much that shapes us into the men and women we will become. Each fingerprint represents purpose, be it entrepreneurial, pioneering, or supportive in nature. No role is too small or too big. We live in a world that is full of diversity. God uses His children in very different ways. One is asked to lay hands on the sick; another speaks the Word; another may just worship and get the same result, and yet another a physician and another a salesman or janitor. Bottom line, we are each an aspect of a larger network of activities designed and engineered by the creator of the universe.

Since we have such diversity and uniqueness amongst us, do not cherish exaggerated ideas of yourself or your importance, but try to have a logical estimate of your capabilities in the light of the faith that God has given you. For just as you have many members in one physical body and those members differ in their functions, so we, though many in number, compose one body in Christ and are all members of one another. Through the grace of God, we have different faculties, gifts, qualities, and talents. If your gift is preaching, then preach to the limit of your vision without competition. If it is serving others, then concentrate on your opportunity to serve;

if it is teaching, give all you have to your teaching assignment; and if your gift be the stimulating of the faith of others, then perfect yourself in it. Let the man who is called to give, give freely; let the man who wields authority think of his responsibility and not come into a place of abuse of power; and let the man who feels sympathy for his fellows act cheerfully.

God is so specific that difference is not the reason for conquest but mutual support. There is no need for competition, no need for envy, no need for slander and certainly no need for murder. Never try to walk in someone else's grace. Be yourself; it is most fulfilling!

The psalmist declared:

Let them now that fear the Lord say, that his mercy endureth for ever. **Psalm 118:4**

O give thanks unto the Lord; for he is good: for his mercy endureth for ever. **Psalm 118:29**

This psalm has so much to say to us. The challenge to pray and remain prayed up from the pulpit or loved ones should never stir up the feeling of guilt but rather a sense of persistence. Prayer is between you and God, so it is a sign that you are committed to your victory when you remain firm on your prayer stance. We have not been called to pray for everyone and for everything.

Grace Requires Relationship

John was the son of a well-to-do businessman. His father was quite open-hearted and considerate. John and his father had built a strong bond in their father-and-son relationship. Whenever John wanted something, regardless of what it was, his father provided for it. He had no reason to deny him anything. John served in the family business and accomplished his fair share of household chores. In the process of time, Sam, a friend of John's, recounted some anxious moments he encountered at home. John quickly told Sam that everything would be all right. "My father will help you," he said. This confidence in his father was fortified by their interaction and love connection.

John's smooth relationship with his father is a form of prayer without demands, and the grace he receives from his father relies on that day-to-day relationship. That relationship, a platform for mutual exchange, has been developed over time and requires that the two invest personal resources in enhancing the forum. It is this kind of relationship that Jesus was introducing when He taught what we have come to call "The Lord's Prayer" (Matthew 6:9-13). Only once in this prayer does Jesus mention asking, and that relates to our daily bread. The rest of the prayer focuses on the relationship between the Father and us: "Our Father who art in Heaven, hallowed be your name. Your kingdom come, your will be done, on earth as it is in heaven. Give us this day our daily bread, and forgive us our debts, as we also have forgiven our debtors. And lead us not into temptation, but deliver us from evil..."

This type of relationship must be the foundation for successfully receiving whatever we ask from God. Ninety percent of our prayer life should be about relating with the Lord and only ten percent of it on asking Him for things we need or want. As God's children, we are also expected to grow in our relationship with Him. How can we do that? You can be in the presence of God when you are in the kitchen, in the shower, or driving your car. The presence of God does not demand a particular location. You can be under attack by thieves or reading a letter that tells you that you are fired, and in both cases, you can also be in the presence of God at the same time.

Natural circumstances should not prevent you from living in God's presence. He is ever present; become aware of this and intentionally incline towards interacting with Him.

Cultivate His Presence

Many people are introduced to God as an answer-generating center. This is why people go from seminar to seminar, healing meeting to healing meeting, prophet to prophet in search of answers. We must be careful that petitioning God does not become the only reason we visit God or care to know Him. Some people go to church based on what they think they can get. Then we don't see them again until the next time they're in trouble. Our reason for being faithful to the household of faith should be to keep hearing more from God and growing in our relationship with Him and with each other.

The need for a constant and ongoing flow of grace brings God's child to a place of total dependence upon Him. Strive to live a life of complete dependence upon Him in every way possible. Every day is a new day and needs its own bread; go for the new and do not capitalize on stale bread and past victories. Don't be deceived; the intensity of your relationship with the Lord determines the vastness and longevity of your victories and conquests.

When David spoke of defeating the bear and the lion, he was careful to give God all the glory. His victories came from his time of fellowship (in praise and worship) with the Lord. He knew that without God, he could not have gone through with the challenges he encountered. He had not done it in his own strength:

David said moreover, The Lord that delivered me out of the paw of the lion, and out of the paw of the bear, he will deliver me out of the hand of this Philistine. **1 Samuel 17:37**

Don't leave God out of the miracle. It would not have happened without His grace. These are His miracles and His testimonies. Give Him thanks:

O give thanks unto the Lord; for he is good: for his mercy endureth for ever. **Psalm 136:1**

You Don't Have to "Deserve" It

When you walk with God, you don't have to "deserve" miracles. The concept of deserving insinuates rewarding someone for a job well done.

27 Then what can we boast about doing to earn our salvation? Nothing at all. Why? Because our acquittal is not based on our good deeds; it is based on what Christ has done and our faith in him. 28 So it is that we are saved by faith in Christ and not by the good things we do. **Romans 3:27-29 (TLB)**

Did the Israelites deserve a miracle when they were wandering in the wilderness for forty years? Not at all! They were constantly murmuring and complaining. But the Lord still walked with them with the pillar by night and by day. It is never about deserving but rather the mercy and goodness of God within His plan and purposes for us. We hear stories of martyred Christians, children of God killed in car accidents and other mishaps. We are not better than they are and neither are they better than we who are still living. No, it is only by grace that you are breathing today. I have known bishops who were in car accidents and died. No doubt all of us have known someone we considered to be very prayerful, and yet they have gone through things that made us wonder and feel sorry for them. If you had to go through those same circumstances, you might not survive them, if you are not on that same spiritual level. But God's grace is available to all.

Let us learn to depend upon His grace. It's not about our visions, our dreams, or the anointing that flows through us. That may all be good in their place, but at the end of the day, it's all about His grace and how we receive it and act upon it.

But the Lord said to Samuel, "Do not look at his appearance or grace his physical stature, because I have refused him. For the Lord does not see as man sees; for man looks at the outward appearance, but the Lord looks at the heart." **1 Samuel 16:7**

23 Search me, O God, and know my heart: try me, and know my thoughts: 24 And see if there be any wicked way in me, and lead me in the way everlasting. **Psalm 139:23**

God's Right to Test You

When dealing with humanity, there is no telling what our hearts have hidden deep within them. It is in times of testing and trials that a man's true nature and state of his heart are revealed. This is also the right timing for transformation because often, a sin uncovered becomes a sin confessed. This is the reason God expects us to be faithful in the little things and also in the greater things. One such great test occurs when one takes on a high seat of enjoyment and then suddenly is handed a broom to clean with all smiles. The most major tests do not happen on our way to the top but rather on our way to the bottom. This is the greatest test because it is at this juncture that our sense of entitlement is tested.

Did you ever study for a test and yet fail it? Did that upset you? Why? Isn't it because you felt entitled to pass? Most of us will agree that when we first came to Christ, things moved quickly; prayers were answered without delay, and we were very conscious of promotion and of everything being good. This beginner's welcome experience seems to change shortly after with the need for fasting and some delayed answers to prayer. Then, when everything around us tells us that we might be below prosperity and advancement, we refuse to believe it. Many children of God who experience bad news hide because we all consider elevated positions to be ones of faith, but that's not true. We need to come out of our self-righteousness and trust in God's saving grace.

Growing up in Ministry

As I was growing up in ministry, I saw amazing signs and wonders. The very first person I laid my hands on (a woman) went out under God's power. I was shocked and a little frightened by this, for I hadn't been expecting it. Fortunately, the woman had already gone under the power of God, or my reaction might have frightened her too. In time, however, this phenomenon became commonplace to me, and I considered it to be the height of ministry experience. Then God began to take me through a transitional period in which He told me not to lay hands on people for a couple of reasons:

1) People falling out had seemed to become the identity of my ministry – There is nothing wrong with people being slain in the spirit, people experiencing outbursts of laughter, shaking under the power of God, having visions, demons crying out of people and leaving, gold dust, being translated to heaven, and other manifestations of the sort. These become an issue when the focus is taken off Jesus, to the man of God and the manifestation to validate the authenticity of the ministry. Please take note that the key word here is "identity."

2) This had begun to raise a lot of talks – There are things that hinder the flow of the Spirit of God such as offense, anger, disobedience, disregard for authority, and speaking ill about others, just to name a few. It is easy to say, "If people want to talk, let them talk," but this is not particularly favorable for you or the

ministry because it leaves negativity in the atmosphere. If it can be avoided, then by all means, do not promote or stir it up.

My problem was pride, however, and when God asked me just to speak the word and in faith expect Him to move, I questioned it: "Why just speak the Word? I need to be laying hands on people." It was more about being seen than it was about people being set free. Such tests can kill us in a minute because ego is seemingly taking precedence over the Spirit. This debate within me created a resistance to the instruction, and unbeknownst to me, I had walked about in rebellion by permitting this word to fall through the cracks and go unexecuted.

That said, every time God teaches us a valuable lesson, as was the case in my next meeting, we remember it. In this next meeting, I laid hands on the first person I prayed for, and the second, but then something happened. Suddenly the atmosphere became dry, tight, and literally closed off, as if God was saying, "Okay, sir, do it by yourself. Do you want to put on a show and be seen? Let's see what you can do alone." I was embarrassed by the results and began to beg God to help me. I felt utterly stripped of power, and I pleaded with Him to return. Thank God for His grace. I soon saw God responding again, not because of me, but because He needed to touch His people. His mercy prevailed. The moment I took myself out of the picture, something hit that service that I can never forget. The glory of God visited each individual, and there were miracles all over the place. Clearly, I saw the difference when I laid hands and when the Lord showed up without me being involved. You must know, as did Moses, having walked with a rod of favor, how to switch to words when God desires it. It is time for His goodness, mercy, and favor. Get ready.

Samson's Grace

After the great exodus from Egypt, the children of God walked through the wilderness to finally settle in the land flowing with milk and honey, as the Lord God had promised them. The family of Israel became a great nation, and God gave them leaders to help resolve the issues that arose among them. Samson was a judge in those days and the last of his kind mentioned in the Book of Judges. According to scripture, he was endowed with strength of enormous proportion with which he put the enemy to flight. In that season, he accomplished things like quickly killing a lion, slaying an entire army with only the jawbone of an ass, and destroying a temple of the Philistines with his bare hands. However, this ability rested on his hair.

One day, out of carelessness with a woman of the Philistines, Delilah, Samson let his guard down, she cut off his long hair, and he lost his strength. At that opportune moment, the enemy attacked, and in response, he woke up and did as at other times, but realized his sin had cost him all the power he possessed. He got up and thought he would do things just as he had done before (Judges 16:20). But it didn't work then, and it won't work today either. None of us owns a pot that cooks up miracles, and since we don't, we need to learn how to go to God in submission, surrender, and worship, asking Him to come to our aid. The Word of God says this kind of prayer will be answered because God will take us on the path of righteousness for His name's sake (Psalm 23:3). He will listen to a broken and contrite heart. God is concerned about His name. He is concerned about His trademark.

The Great Comeback!

In the story mentioned above, a summation of the life of Samson the Judge and his mighty fall, we see the tragedy that befalls us when we do not match the grace of God with proportionate character expectations. The child of God must be aware of the dangers that surround the saints and live a life that repels as many attempts as possible sent by the enemy of our soul. With that said, blessed be the LORD Almighty, who will not suffer us to remain in the abyss but will come to our rescue because the full price has been paid for redemption. The demise of Samson cost him his vision (eyes removed), his strength (hair cut), and they put him in prison and made him work grinding grain; working for the enemy he was to put away, he became the reason for laughter and mockery as they used him for sport.

The Philistine rulers came together to celebrate. They were going to offer a great sacrifice to their god, Dagon. They said, "Our god helped us defeat Samson, our enemy." When the Philistines saw Samson, they praised their god. They said, "This man destroyed our people! He killed many of our people! But our god helped us take our enemy!" The people were having a good time at the celebration and said, "Bring Samson out. We want to make fun of him." So they brought Samson from the prison and made fun of him. They made him stand between the columns in the temple of the god Dagon. While all of this was going on, the Bible says: "BUT HIS HAIR BEGAN TO GROW!" God of mercy, grace, full of love and purpose, began to grow Samson's hair without consulting with anyone. Come on, Jesus! Yes, that is right, without consulting with anyone either. Do you see God growing your hair too, from that place of shame and failure, from that place of sin and guilt? Your hair is growing! Probably like the case of Samson, no one including you is noticing, but KNOW and UNDERSTAND that God is working behind the scenes for your restoration.

One More Time!

This statement reveals within it a cry of desperation and a longing for validation. Everything that was happening made Samson appreciate and value his God, and an internal hatred grew within him for the enemy. The people were having a good time at the celebration and said, "Bring Samson out. We want to make fun of him." So they brought Samson from the prison and made fun of him. This mockery wasn't just about Samson but also about his God. "Where is your God now and where is your might?" Oh yes, it all boils down to this. When we fall and neglect the grace of God, it is not only about us. The entire kingdom pays for the error, while darkness rejoices.

They made him stand between the columns in the temple of the god Dagon. A servant was holding his hand. Samson said to him, "Put me where I can feel the pillars that hold this temple up. I want to lean against them." The temple was crowded with men and women. All the Philistine rulers were there. There were about

3,000 men and women on the roof of the temple. They were laughing and making fun of Samson. Then Samson said a prayer to the Lord. "Lord God, remember me. God, please give me strength one more time. Let me do this one thing to punish these Philistines for tearing out both of my eyes!" This prayer was not only timely for Samson but is timely for you right NOW.

Think back on all the injustices that were done to you, all the evil in the world, the many soldiers—valiant men and women who have taken the sidewalk, injured and confused; it is time to ask for a revival and fire upon the laborers. Arise and ask God for another move of His Spirit upon the land. Pray as if it all depends on you!

Samson took hold of the two pillars in the center of the temple that supported the whole temple. He braced himself between the two columns. One column was at his right side and the other on his left side. Samson said, "Let me die with these Philistines!" Then he pushed as hard as he could, and the temple fell on the authorities and everyone in it. In this way, Samson killed more Philistines on the day of his death than all the days he was alive.

Our Father is a God of many chances. Do not only ask for one and stop; ask yet for another and again another until Jesus comes. Do not quit so early; **do not bargain with death in mind. You can win and celebrate the victory.** No death until the time set by the LORD. Oh LORD, GIVE ME ANOTHER MOVE OF YOUR SPIRIT IN JESUS' NAME!

The Power of God's Grace

You can see the power of God's grace in Psalm 136. Please take the time to read it and contemplate its truths. For example, did you ever think about what the stretching of the earth has to do with God's mercy (Psalm 136:6)? It was in this same psalm that David referred to the parting of the Red Sea:

To him which divided the Red Sea into parts: for his mercy endureth for ever: and made Israel pass through the midst of it: for his mercy endureth for ever. **Psalm 136:13-14**

The saving grace of God will cause Him to divide the Red Sea on your behalf, too. He will have people fired from their position and put you in their place because His mercy endures forever. It's a twist. One person suffers, while another is in joy, just because God's mercy is upon the individual who is in joy. He can show you the questions that will be on an exam you are about to take, because His mercy endures forever. He will pay your bills although you have been spending all your money, because His mercy endures forever. He will save you from an accident even though you have not been driving well, because His mercy endures forever.

I'm sure you know some people who did things and escaped and others who did the same and got caught. Some women or men and young girls or boys who got involved in sexual ventures at a time they were not supposed to and no one became pregnant, neither did they contract any disease. Despite all the exposure, God's mercy prevailed, for it endures forever. You applied for a job and didn't have the requirements, yet when the selection was made, they picked you. Why? Because God's mercy endures forever. Rules and regulations can be changed at your place of work just because God has mercy on you. It is time for the people of God to lift up their hands and bless Him because His mercy endures forever. The violent take God's Kingdom by force (Matthew 11:12) because His mercy endures forever. We can now talk about David as a man after God's own heart, because God's mercy endures forever. The man Moses survived out of many babies who were killed, because God's mercy endures forever. It's all about God's mercy. Now it's up to us to decide to walk in this grace He so freely offers us. Stop now and shout it: *Grace! Grace!*

"To be grateful is to recognize the Love of God in everything He has given us—and He has given us everything. Every breath we draw is a gift of His love, every moment of existence is a grace, for it brings with it immense graces from Him. Gratitude therefore takes nothing for granted, is never unresponsive, is constantly awakening to new wonder and to praise of the goodness of God. For the grateful person knows that God is good, not by hearsay but by experience. And that is what makes all the difference."

– Thomas Merton

CHAPTER 5

Grace that Keeps on Gracing!

The young lions do lack, and suffer hunger: but they that seek the Lord shall not want any good thing. **Psalm 34:10**

In this chapter, I want us to look at another reality regarding God's grace. We will be discussing the growing potential of the grace of God. Are you open for more grace? There is such a thing as the measure of grace. For this to be understood, we need to bring into account the principles of the Kingdom of God. The Word of God depicts the Kingdom of God as being like a seed. In Mark 4, scripture declares that our comprehension of the Parable of the Seed and the Sower is paramount to understanding the workings of the Kingdom of God itself. This makes the parable of supreme importance to us. Back in the Book of Zechariah, we hear the Spirit of the Lord telling us not to despise the days of small beginnings

(Zechariah 4:10), because to the little you have, more can be added. Are you ready for more grace? Let's begin.

Substituting Grace with Grain

For a moment, I want to replace the word grace with the word grain. So my question now becomes: "Are you ready for more grain?" If seeds are put into the ground, they will multiply, so when we talk about more grace, we are talking about putting grace to use for more production of grace. We want to create more than we have produced thus far.

The apostle James has a way of telling us that we can't sit on our words, alluding to the fact that faith without works is dead. We must combine actions with our words and aspirations. You can't sit on your dreams. Faith without works is dead. Stepping out and taking the first steps in the journey of obedience and fulfillment is the magic component that turns the faucet of the grace of God loose over us. All desired dreams will remain as unrealized pictures until you begin to make a move. You can't sit on your vision. It will just be a mental image, until you start acting accordingly. You must put strategy and legs to your vision if it will ever come to pass. We are under a God who gives more grain. It's up to us to seek it. It is in working out our vision or assignment that we begin to experience the multiple levels of grace allocated to us. **Each adventure leaves a trail of knowledge, and with more awareness comes the opportunity to experience more grace.**

"Take Heed"

Mark records Jesus telling us that "things are hidden temporarily only as a means to revelation. For there is nothing hidden except to be revealed, nor is anything temporarily kept secret except so that it may be made known." Besides, He said, "Be careful what you are hearing," because the measure of thought and study you give to the truth you hear will be the quantity of virtue and knowledge that comes back to you—and more besides will be given to you who hear. "For to him who has will more be given; and from him who has nothing, even what he has will be taken away by force." We become the gospel we listen to most of the time, and behave like what we keep hearing most of the time. Grace is multiplied to you through the knowledge of God and of Jesus Christ (2 Peter 1:2).

And he said unto them, Take heed what ye hear: with what measure ye mete, it shall be measured to you: and unto you that hear shall more be given. **Mark 4:24**

When the truth of this verse first hit my spirit, I read it over and over again, and each time I read it, I was amazed. God is telling us that there is Someone who responds to what we do and gives back to us proportionately to the amount we vested. Our actions are like seeds, and there is Someone who is watching all we do, watching how we manage our seed, and He knows how to come and water that seed.

To the Corinthians, Paul wrote:

I have planted, Apollos watered; but God gave the increase. **1 Corinthians 3:6**

The increase comes from God and nowhere else. In Acts, we see God adding to the church such as needed to be saved (Acts 2:47). As we now explore this whole concept, may God open our eyes to the grace that keeps on gracing, and add more grace to us according to our hunger and desire for His workings.

I call this "grace that keeps on gracing" because this grace manifests in continuous increments with each and every day, and takes us from one level to another. Like a building that develops one brick at a time, the Word of God tells us that it shall be "line upon line and precept upon precept" (Isaiah 28:10, 13). Throughout the Scriptures, we find this construction concept taking place because God is in the business of giving, and He is ready to give much more than we have ever received.

Receiving Life More Abundantly

John records Jesus speaking of giving us life and giving us "life... more abundantly" (John 10:10). God's favorite thing is to give us more. So the question is: are you ready and open for more grace? The answer to this inquiry would not be a yes, without the willingness to work. Why want more if *more* has no intended use? If you are available to utilize more grace, God is available to give more of it. His Word declares:

If any of you lack wisdom, let him ask of God, that giveth to all men liberally, and upbraideth not; and it shall be given him. **James 1:5**

Grace that Keeps on Gracing!

The Amplified Bible says it this way:

If any of you is deficient in wisdom, let him ask of the giving God [Who gives] to everyone liberally and ungrudgingly, without reproaching or faultfinding, and it will be given him.

That is our God!

When we talk about giving and going an extra mile in giving even more, we can easily see that God doesn't give grudgingly. He wants to give abundantly. You and I, as recipients, literally determine how much more of His grace comes to us. There is an infinite source out of which we can obtain an unlimited supply of everything that pertains to life and godliness. He wants to open the windows and let His grace flow down upon us, but it's up to us to settle for His assistance, open our arms wide, and flow with HIM.

Open to More Finances

So many are very uncomfortable talking about money (let alone more finances) that it has almost become unnatural to suggest that God and money can be in the same sentence. The silver and the gold belong to the Lord. So concerning finances, you need to open yourself up for more. If you do, God will use you as an excellent conduit to channel funds wherever needed. Remember the Word of God says that He who waters must first be watered (Proverbs 11:25). This scripture reveals the basics of getting more. If with your assignment you are watered because you watered one person, logic, therefore, indicates that to increase your level of watering, just reach out to more people. This is more like the law of compensation: You are rewarded for your efforts and the value of your services in equal proportion. God will not allow the ox that treads the corn to be muzzled (1 Corinthians 9:9 and 1 Timothy 5:8). Why? Because the bull can't trample the corn with its mouth closed. It must eat of that same corn. This means that you can't play with water and not get wet. You can't play with fire and not get burned. If you have God's grace upon your life, that grace will keep on gracing you more and more. The formula for more is:

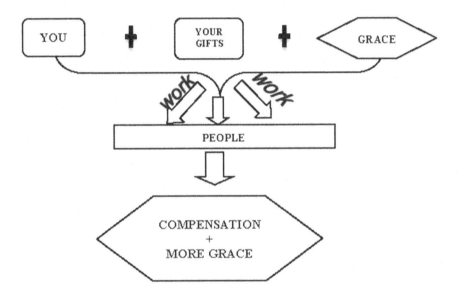

You and Your Gift + Grace ----- People = Compensation and More Grace and the cycle goes on and on.

The grace that keeps gracing operates similarly to a magnet. It can attract one blessing, and just as easily draw in another. For us to access this grace, we must

1) Desire it and open ourselves to it, and

2) Understand how it comes.

God's Will Should Motivate All Our Asking

These days, shopping for anything is becoming increasingly comfortable considering all the options at the consumer's disposal. We have department stores that carry distinct items, and you can also go online, check on what aisle an item is found, pay for it, and either pick it up or have it shipped to you. Amazing how this world is, like they say, becoming a global village. It is all good for the consumer because time is preserved for other things. Imagine for a minute what would happen if you went to a car parts shop to buy household furniture, or you went to an electronics store to purchase tickets for a football game. Just out of place, right? Consider that God has the same system: departments, specified merchandise, time of operation, high-end and low-end consideration for products and so on, all working according to His omnipotent architectural plan.

If we have to deal with God and have our prayers answered with less stress and confusion involved, we will need to ask considering God's will in mind, and not our own ideology or lust. "And this is the confidence that we have in him, that, if we ask anything according to his will, he heareth us: And if we know that he hear us, whatsoever we ask, we know that we have the petitions that we desired of him. You ask and do not receive, because you ask amiss, that you may spend *it* on your pleasures" (1 John 5:14-15 and James 4:3). The reason we don't get the desired results or hit the intended target is that our focus is wrong. So, James is saying, if anyone wants to have prayers answered, they cannot focus on themselves. Instead, they must focus on where the flow is coming from (God) and where it is going (God's will). The day we take our focus off the Source and the end result, we will be asking "amiss."

You cannot continually receive without purpose. When you keep taking without a plan, the items will be misused, and you will have missed God's order. God isn't trying to give you more so that you store it in addition to what you already have. He is giving you more so that you can make proper use of it. The reason you don't receive is that you ask "amiss." This defectiveness is principally the result of wrong thinking—engaging in self-focus or self-gratification. If you want to walk in grace that keeps on gracing, forget yourself, and focus on purpose and the Source. If you fail to concentrate on these two, you will be cut off from obtaining results and won't realize that you have cut yourself off.

Holes in Your Bucket

My parents told us stories while growing up as a way of conveying lasting moral lessons. One such story spoke of a father who lived miles up a hill. Streams surrounded the countryside village, and the indigenes used these waters for their everyday water needs. One day, the children of this man decided to bore holes through his buckets so that he would not send them out to get water. They hated and considered it tedious climbing the hilly countryside carrying buckets of water. In their minds, if they burst these holes, there would be nothing to hold water and so they could rest from this tough menial job. When their father realized what had been done, and figured out the evil behind this plot, he called them together and said, "Today you will fill all the water jars to the brim so that you can take a break for the week. So get going and get the water in." If only they had known, they would not have done this evil because now that they had a week off, it would be almost impossible to fetch water and transport it safely because they had put holes in the buckets.

When walking with grace and planning for more grace, we have to endeavor not to bore holes in the same bucket that will sustain us. Like Jesus said, "No one will do such miracles who will lightly speak evil of me." If you are going to climb the corporate ladder and make it to the top on your journey, decide today not to speak ill of your boss. If you do such things, you have already fired yourself, a dead man walking, so to speak.

You can't expect to be fruitful in something you are tearing down. You cannot receive from what you don't respect, esteem, or value. Everything you will ever get in life will be given to you by someone. There is always a price to pay to walk into a particular realm or position. It will be hard to receive if we do not develop the disposition of honor and respect for those who have gone ahead of us.

So, when we talk about abiding in God's grace, we are referring to the notion of walking in an awareness of the Source, the direction of His flow, and last but not least, the season set for manifestation. When you know these things, it makes all the difference, and you will undoubtedly receive.

Judgment Based on Today or the Future?

Very often, people sink into depression because all they see around them is a lack of life, as in unfulfilled dreams, or overestimate themselves because they have the wrong view of their real world. This is all the work of perception: it makes all the difference in a sad day or joyous day. Perception is everything; it determines what we see, how we see it, and ultimately what we do with it.

There is a story often told by the ancient about the cat that ran away from the mouse that had fallen in a glass of red wine. After consuming most of the contents in the glass, the mouse jumped out of the glass. At the same instant, a cat was standing right there ready to devour it. The mouse, in its drunken state, perceived the cat as its reflection and concluded, "I am as strong and as mighty as what I see," so it forged forward. Meanwhile, on the other side of things, the cat thought, "This mouse isn't scared of me. Something is definitely different about this one. I have lost my sight." As the mouse approached with its red drunken eyes, the cat turned and ran away for fear there was a lion coming after it. If you have the wrong perception, you will run away from an anthill thinking it is a mountain, or eat sand thinking it is rice.

If you are viewing your life and checking on the things that you have today as the sum total of that life, then you are totally mistaken. Today's possessions do not define you; today is simply the result of all that happened yesterday; today is here to show you what you are to change and grow from. Your real life is still miles ahead of you on the date called future. There is a future you are coming from. A day eye has not seen, possessing testimonies that ear has not heard, and yet all is in the heart of God ready to be re-vealed by His Spirit in us.

When you are defining yourself, do not do it from the stand-point of your current circumstance, past errors, or projected suc-cess. It should be based on the prophecy that is gone ahead of you. Paul advised Timothy, his son, instructing him to war in life based on the divine predictions that had gone ahead of him (1 Timothy 1:18). This way his warfare would be successful. When many peo-ple are asked about their well-being, they respond in such a man-ner that renders the one who inquires sad and feeling depressed for them. That's because they are defining themselves on account of the present-day circumstance, rather than speaking from the platform of the grace or greatness God is applying to their lives.

If you define yourself based on your today, you will also define others based on their today. Due to the limited nature of such defi-nition, you may never see far into the future of countless individu-als around you. That isn't the principle of the Kingdom. Greater is He that is in us than he that is in the world. Listen, you are a million times bigger on the inside than on the outside. Let people talk and think they can take you down. They are just looking at your exte-rior, for you are a million times bigger on the inside than you are on the outside. Regardless of the challenges you may face, the failures you may have encountered, and whatever else the future holds, the end of this script is already written; God knew the end before He started you. Trust in GRACE, for He is coming through for you. He that is with you is greater and bigger. He is all sufficient. Though the ride may be bumpy, the Rider is also the way. Rest in HIM!

Finally, Now You Can

Don't Get Hosed!

My wife Pauline works with some special people who are occasionally hosed because they refuse to take showers. I asked her
if that hurts, and she said it does. I asked if she had done it before
herself, and she said yes. "I have yet to see a man or woman who
will go under the hose and excitedly jump up and down, thanking
us for water," she relayed. How sad!

This seems to be a perfect picture that relays our behavior
towards abundance. It is too much and comes too fast, and so
our minds cry out foul, unusual, and as a result, uncomfortable.
Abundance is something people are afraid of. I know individuals
who are scared of being loved, afraid of acknowledgment, or afraid
of any extra attention. If you are afraid to have more, then this message is for you.

More than 90 Percent Are Fearful of Having More

More than 90 percent of the people on the face of the earth
today are frightened by the thought of having more. How do I know
this? Because the wealth of the world is in the hands of the other
10 percent. The richest individuals make up just 3 percent. Why are
these people so wealthy? If you took their wealth and gave it to the
90 percent, they would quickly squander it.

Surveys show that there are a variety of reasons that people
waste their money. Some do it because they are unsure of what
opportunities tomorrow might hold. Others do it because they

suddenly have the chance of owning something they have desired for a very long time. Others are frankly afraid that they can't handle it or handle it well. They self-sabotage and default to their most comfortable state—not having enough—and that brings a sigh of relief because it seems to feel right inside.

It is incredible how much people fear to have more and how much that fear puts them in bondage. The Word of God tells us that everyone who is afraid to die spends their lifetime in prison. How interesting! When you are afraid, you can't leave the confines of that jail. And, consequently, you can never become wealthy.

Check around and see how many years it takes to get a degree from a good school. Not many. And yet many people are challenged in working toward a degree that will open doors of opportunity to them. It reveals the crippling effects of fear.

Is Merit Overrated?

Every coin is two-sided. Each of these sides brings relevance to the other, and together they make up the coin. The curse upon humanity brings with it the discrepancies of the human being. We now live in a realm that is influenced by the Law as well as by grace. On one side of this system, the rule is:

Whatever you do, be it right or wrong, you will obtain an equivalent compensation for your actions down to future generations.

While on the other side of the system, the rule is:

All requirements have been satisfied—paid in full; all shortcomings forgiven; acknowledge the payee; side with Him and you will receive the compensation.

To demonstrate this, let us consider the following story found in Luke, chapter 5. It all happened one day as Jesus was preaching on the shore of Lake Gennesaret, and great crowds pressed in on him to listen to the Word of God. He noticed two empty boats at the water's edge while the fishermen washed their nets. Stepping into one of the boats, Jesus asked Simon, its owner, to push out a little into the water so that he could sit in the ship and speak to the crowds from there.

When he had finished speaking, he said to Simon, "Now go out where it is deeper and let down your nets and you will catch a lot of fish!"

"Sir," Simon replied, "we worked hard all last night and didn't get a thing. But if you say so, we'll try again." And this time the net was so full that it began to tear! They called to their friends in the other boat to help them. The friends came, and both boats were filled so full of fish that they were almost sinking. When Simon Peter realized what had happened, he fell to his knees before Jesus and said, "Oh, sir, please leave us—I'm too much of a sinner for you to have around." For he was awestruck by the size of their catch, as were the others with him, and his partners too—James and John, the sons of Zebedee. Jesus replied, "Don't be afraid! From now on you'll be fishing for the souls of men!"

In this amazing account of God providing fish, Peter, the professional fisherman, is saying, "I am a sinful man; I don't know it all, and blunder on the things I am knowledgeable about; errors are weaved in my performance." On account of merit, Peter had failed and had no grounds for expecting anything. Deserving requires that one meets all criteria, and this wasn't Peter's story.

Grace did not come for the worthy but for the unmeriting. The call for holiness is our ultimate destination, and making strides towards it, grace is the glue and balm that connects us to the next height and expectation of supremacy. We need to build a generation that believes they can attain what they haven't earned. It's God's time. Believe that you can marry that high-profile person, if that is what God is saying to you. You can get that dream job, yes, you can walk in spiritual gifts of healing and deliverance though you failed to pray for twelve hours. You will find yourself attaining levels you haven't earned. Grace will close in on the gaps.

Merit is great, but it isn't an absolute. You can be gifted with a paid-off house, a car you did not buy; indeed, by the grace of God, you will be favored and settled. That's possible, and it is coming to pass. Faith isn't a commodity used in the rewarding or sowing and reaping realm but rather in the realm of grace. Faith isn't based on what you look like or how much training you have received. Faith is taking on the stronger God with you in a covenant relationship to assist you in meeting all shortcomings.

Stop Putting Yourself Down

When people give us a funny look or make derogatory comments about us, we are quick to jump on them and ask them not to look at us like that ever again, but we are rarely that quick to look at ourselves or talk to ourselves in the same manner.

In fact, I have noticed a trend among most people, and it might be your case too. There is such a thing as your inner critic. It is that voice lodged deep in your head that judges you, belittles you, doubts you, and regularly tells you that you are up to no good. It picks from the past, the present, and the environment around to analyze and call you inadequate. It says negative, harmful, and poisonous things to you—things that you would otherwise never tell another person—such as "I am such an empty head; I am so stupid; I never get anything right; I will never make it."

Recognize it or not, everything you say to yourself matters. The inner critic isn't innocent. It prohibits you, limits you, and stops you from pursuing the life you absolutely want to live. It strips you of peace of mind and emotional well-being. I remember someone asking me this question once. "Sir," she said, "what if the inner voice is right on every count?" Believe me; this is a great question. For some reason, the question made me laugh because I could instantly recognize the irony in a deception. For anyone to be effectively deceived, the lie must in every way come across as true, very convincing, and the plot will become tangible.

Now, listen! Right or wrong is not the point here. We need to recognize that negative self-talk is never in your interest. There is always a better, different, kinder way to treat yourself that does not involve derogatory labels and a self-destructive mindset. In any given situation, you can always focus on what you did wrong or what you did well or even better, what you can improve on next time. Just don't stop; keep it moving and keep building.

If you tell yourself something negative, confront your inner self with creative words from the scriptures asserting who you are in Christ Jesus, and that storm will be banished.

We need to rise above a regular hourly wage. It's time that we speak somewhere for thirty minutes, and the entire company is so transformed that we leave that place with a check for $30,000 and why not more. The people who are doing that are no different from you. When you speak positively or better yet scripturally to yourself, you create a better you in alignment with God's agenda for your life. There is more to you than meets the eye. Stop putting yourself down! Build yourself in your most holy faith. Know you are more, understand you will be more, and see yourself at the level of more. The best is yet to come! Of course, this truth is not limited to money. That's just one of the aspects of it. What about much more love? Much more respect? Much more mercy? Much more forgiveness? Much more goodness? You need to expect all of that and more.

For this to come your way, you need to come to an understanding of the meaning behind the words of the proverb:

A man that hath friends must shew himself friendly: and there is a friend that sticketh closer than a brother. **Proverbs 18:24**

Let us develop a lifestyle that exhibits a mindset of "not caring about the size of a tree, but about its depth in the ground." Do not disregard the days of small beginnings. Regardless of where you are in life, deepen your roots, and when it is time for the fruits, they will come through naturally. The scripture is saying, if anyone wants anything, the person must first BE the thing he seeks so that he can

ATTRACT what he seeks. In conclusion, to HAVE more, YOU must BE-come MORE. In other words, when we come to BE more, then we have COME to more.

God "Giveth More Grace"

But he giveth more grace. Wherefore he saith, God resisteth the proud, but giveth grace unto the humble. **James 4:6**

The obvious conclusion is that the humbler you are, the more grace will increase in your life. The meeker you become, the more God will visit you.

Strangely many are unwilling to submit to His will. You could not be a good student and pass an exam without submitting to the teacher who also must test you. If you refuse to comply with the teacher's training schedule, you will fail that program. You won't even get to take the test. Submit to God, and He will give you "more grace."

This is a principle of the Kingdom of God. If we have "some," that "some" can increase. With "some" comes "more," and that is the order for spiritual progress. More may mean something deeper and higher. Just get more. Pray this prayer with me:

Father, find in me someone faithful for more. In the name of Jesus.

Grace that Keeps on Gracing!

Wherever you are, be it in a public venue or your vehicle driving alone or with people, pull over, take this moment seriously, excuse yourself, and just shout out:

More grace!

Grace! Grace!

Grace! Grace!

Grace! Grace!

In Jesus' name,

Amen!

"Rising above mediocrity never just happens; it's always a result of faith combined with works. Faith without works is like gold within the earth. It is of no value until it is mined. A person who has faith but no actions is like a bird that has wings but no feet. The Bible says, 'Faith by itself, if it does not have works, is dead' (James 2:17 NKJV). Biblical principles multiplied by nothing equal nothing. Let's be people who put our faith into action. One individual with faith and action constitutes a majority."

— John Mason

CHAPTER 6

Grace that Does Not Derail

Even when I don't know where I am supposed to go or what to do, the Lord shepherds me. And I will get to my allotted destination because He leads me. This statement has locked within it the mystery of stability. As it clearly says, your destination is secure because He is leading you. As we dive in to this chapter, I want you to understand and accept this right off the bat. To be derailed means to be accidentally or intentionally diverted from the intended course. Now, since we are talking about staying the course, kindly consider Newton's First Law of Motion, which states, "A body at rest will remain at rest, and a body in motion will remain in uniform motion in a straight line, unless it is compelled to change that state when acted upon by an external force." This simply means that things cannot start, stop, or change direction all by themselves. It takes some force, acting on them from the outside, to cause such a change. If you have ever been derailed, clearly something external set you off on a course that might or might not have been your intended route.

So what do I mean by the "grace that does not derail"? This is the operation of grace upon an individual not just to keep them stable, but also to ensure that they arrive at their intended destination. This is the mystery locked in the twenty-third Book of Psalms.

To drive this point home, consider an individual who goes out shopping. They may have plans to buy groceries, food items, or clothing. In the course of shopping, they will use a basket or push a shopping cart around to help them transport the items they will buy. When they see something they want or need, they will pick it up and put it in the basket or cart.

In a similar way, we are like a shopping cart in God's hand. He knows what we need and when we need it. I will not worry or be bothered about what is supposed to be for me (as a cart) because as He carries me around, He will put in me exactly what needs to be there. No shopping cart says, "Put groceries or clothing in me now." It relies on the one who handles it, and God is our shepherd. He is our handler. He knows the number of our hairs, the length of our days, the enemy's plans, our weaknesses and strengths. Permit Him to take the wheel of your life and refrain from the temptation of interrupting His leading.

There are two main streams of knowledge, science and religion, and both of them proceed from the Source of ALL KNOWLEDGE— God. Please do not consider it abstract that I use science to prove divine intelligence. Science is God's creation and not His enemy. It is only the user of either the Bible or science that makes things seem bad or negative.

In the beginning of this chapter, I mentioned Newton's Law of Motion. This law brings into play three major considerations to any type of motion—force, mass, and acceleration, all of which need time to bring definition to their definition. Take a journey with me now through the scriptures as we look at the life of Paul and his concept of grace and we attempt to bring relevance to our concept.

Respect God's Timing

Let us begin this section with the respect of timing with which all things are tested. There are many people to whom God has promised things, but who rush ahead of Him because they became impatient. **The grace of God works within the timing of God.** When we rush or do things because the promise has not yet materialized, we begin to create things outside the "grace zone."

Consider for a minute the miracle of you becoming the next well-known evangelist, or the next prominent businessman or woman, or even the next president. It takes more than just you in the picture to make such miracles possible. God, by His grace, has to touch several other people. Many around the world are also as human as you get to be all the time, and so could exhibit dis-obedient tendencies, sluggish mannerisms, and other emotional hazards which slow down progress. With that said, such miracles may require years of smaller miracles, which together create the big miracle. Timing is major! That is the reason we hear statements like "God's timing is the best." In His timing, grace is released; all things become beautiful.

Think about it. Suppose that Mary had become pregnant before she was mature enough to handle it. She could not have said: *"Be it unto me according to thy word"* **(Luke 1:38).** The grace of God has a timing clause to it, and once we are sensitive to the timing of God, we will be able to walk in His grace. In the meantime, we must not suffer from impatience as we are waiting for God's grace. The grace for waiting on the Lord also keeps the child of God worry-free during the waiting period. The grace of God not only demands that the child of God waits on God before making a move, but also maintains the child of God in a composed state while enduring the process of waiting. There is peace in the storm while we wait for deliverance—this is the power of grace made available to all.

Waiting on God's Grace

The Word talks about *"the peace of God that passeth all understanding"* (Philippians 4:7).

Someone may question you, saying: "Why don't you do this thing or that thing?" and you reply, "No, not yet, I am waiting on God. I don't feel quite yet that I should." The other person may not understand that what you are actually saying is that you are waiting for His grace. Once the grace of God is released, then you are able to function without using your own strength. If the grace of God comes upon you for a particular job, you will find favor for that job. If not, you will struggle or, at best, proceed with human abilities.

Right about now you might be wondering if your current hardships or struggles, in general, are an indication of the absence of God's grace. Yes and no! As Jesus would say to His disciples, "I have told you these things, so that in me you may have peace. In this world, you will have trouble: many trials and sorrows. But take heart! I have overcome the world." The proper behavior toward every challenge or test is to count it all joy (to read more on this subject, refer to Chapter 11, "Activate Grace Through Praise"). Therefore, struggles, in themselves, are not necessarily an indication of an absence of grace from God. "Peace I leave with you; My peace I give to you. I do not give to you as the world gives. Do not let your hearts be troubled; do not be afraid." The instruction here is "Do not let your hearts be troubled!" The grace to take us through is present and so, do not permit solicitude to infiltrate your being. It is a destructive spirit whose intention is to rob you of your promised land; give it no place!

I need to bring balance to this point, for this has raised a serious question that many of us have had to deal with, either in ourselves or in others: Do folded arms necessarily indicate waiting on God? No! In the movie *Failure to Launch*, a grown man has an inability to settle, live on his own, get married, and have a life that does not require his parents' 100 percent support. This isn't waiting on God's grace, but rather a behavior of clumsiness.

The waiter at the restaurant waits on the tables. He observes while attending to customers—supplying them with food and drink as requested. A server takes on a crucial role in a restaurant, which is to always be attentive and accommodating to the guests. As you can see, waiting is not the absence of functionality, but the presence of deep, sincere dedication to the service of the Master. While we wait, we worship, we praise, we serve, we come to the aid of others, we listen, we obey, we yield, and we do it all in joy. Please understand that "released grace" is not necessarily a tangible thing that you can touch or feel—as in a spark, kick, voice, shock, or nudge—but a strength that you walk into as you venture out.

In conclusion, whatever we do or whatever opportunities knock at our door, waiting shouldn't be a period of folded arms or sitting down doing nothing, but rather a time of carrying out small steps leading to the major steps to come.

Understanding the Grace of God in Others

In this portion of the teaching, we shall be talking about the application or use of the grace of God when dealing with other humans or children of God. Scripture says: our knowledge is partial and incomplete, and even the gift of prophecy reveals only part of the whole picture, so this is a very sensitive and slippery slope. There are times when you will not only have to understand the grace of God in someone else's life, but you will also have to accept it, just as he or she will have to comprehend and accept the grace of God upon your life. We have not been permitted to be validators of the grace of God upon someone, but we need to flow with others in the bond of unity.

Responding Urgently

Paul wrote:

But when it pleased God, who separated me from my mother's womb, and called me by his grace, to reveal his Son in me, that I might preach him

among the heathen; immediately I conferred not with flesh and blood.
Galatians 1:15-16

Did you notice the word *immediately* in the verse of scripture? This is not the first time this expression was used in the Scriptures. This kind of urgency was frequently communicated in the Word of God. Throughout the book of Matthew, for example, you can see words like *suddenly* and *immediately* used to describe people's rush to obey God, or God's rapid response to a healing or deliverance situation.

The Bible says that one day, while James and John were fishing, Jesus called out to them, and they *immediately* got off their boat and followed Him (Matthew 4:22). When you are tuned into the grace of God, you will know how to follow the Lord and the biddings of grace suddenly. We must all know how to act promptly and on time. Wasting precious time can cause the grace of God to pass you by.

In **Zechariah 4:6**, the Bible says*:*

Not by might, nor by power, but by my spirit, saith the Lord of hosts.

God is ready. Are you? You should always want to be in grace's timing because everything that the Spirit of the Lord does is perfect, just as He declares in His Word:

The Lord will perfect that which concerneth me. **Psalm 138:8**

Paul continued the thought:

Immediately I conferred not with flesh and blood: neither went I up to Jerusalem to them which were apostles before me. **Galatians 1:16-17**

Most of us like receiving confirmations on things that the Lord has told us or things that we would like to pursue. If a person wants to get into the field of nursing, for example, they will talk to as many nurses as possible. Some, however, after talking with dozens of nurses, still feel the need for more confirmation. You could speak with a thousand and one nurses, but at some point, you should make a decisive move, without which that would be counterproductive. Know when you have done enough research. Discern when to stop investigating and start moving forward. There is such a thing as a grace window: a window of opportunity, if you will, with which to act and/or get things done.

"Go"

One day God visited Jeremiah and told him to go to the potter's house, for there he would be able to receive a message (Jeremiah 18). We are not told what Jeremiah was doing at the moment, but we know that Jeremiah obeyed God, regardless of what he had been doing. He did not say, "God, let me finish my laundry first." Clearly, his response was not "Hold on a minute. Let me complete my cooking." God told him to go to the potter's house, and he went to the potter's house. Period!

According to the story, when Jeremiah got to the potter's house, he observed what the potter was doing; how he formed vessels on his wheel. He had just finished his work on one vessel, and it had not turned out well. Immediately he picked it back up and began to rework it until he was able to produce a perfect vessel.

After a while, God spoke to Jeremiah. *"Now I want you to go and tell the people of Israel that in the same way the potter took the malformed vessel and reshaped it until it became lovely and useful, so I will do with them."* What would have happened to this prophetic word if Jeremiah for some reason took his time and arrived sometime later at the potter's house? Timing is everything. When God says, "Go," then we need to go.

You and I must know how to deal with the timing of God, the grace of God, and the imperfect human beings we encounter every day. This understanding and way of doing things is paramount to our maximum success and God's continual release of grace.

Paul's Walk of Grace

Paul, who walked in grace, had a revelation of grace that led him to take the steps he took in his life and ministry. We know that when he was first saved, he "did not confer with flesh and blood." Then some time passed, and he said: "But I went into Arabia, and returned again unto Damascus." He continued:

Then after three years, I went up to Jerusalem to see Peter, and abode with him fifteen days. **Galatians 1:18**

Now Paul knew what he had to do. God had shown him that he had a special assignment to perform, and Paul said, "Yes." On the spot, he set his mind to obey the heavenly vision.

Obedience Starts in Your Heart

Obedience does not start with an action; it starts in your heart. Actions only reveal what you have already settled to do within you. There are those who say, "Yes, I will obey," but their actions say otherwise. Then there are those who don't really feel like doing what God is saying, but they love Him so much that, even though they may stumble at times, they remain on the path to doing what God has asked them to do. **Obedience, then, is primarily the state of one's heart.** If the Word of God has not touched your heart, all your attempts to do His bidding will end in your brain.

When you sit under a preaching of the Word of God, the tendency is to analyze the message delivered, and settle within you how to proceed with the demands and/or requirements of the Holy Scriptures. Obeying the Word of God is something you need to resolve to do, regardless of what the requests are. As a child of God, your greatest desire is to conform to the Father's will. Obedience that proceeds from the heart solely emanates from a disposition of humility, loyalty, and an unwavering pursuit of perfection. There must be a profound desire to become aligned to the creative process of the Lord, for in Him we live, move, and have our being. May your heart DICTATE and command an uncompromising walk of obedience.

The Effect of Christ

In **Galatians 2:21**, which says, *"I do not frustrate the grace of God: for if righteousness come by the law, then Christ is dead in* *vain,"* God caused me to read the verse without including the middle statement that says, "for if righteousness come by the law."

When I began my study on the grace of God, the Lord reminded me of the wording of the same scripture in the New King James Version of the Bible, which says: *"I do not set aside the grace of God; ...then Christ died in vain."* Look at it in your own Bible. Take out the middle phrase, and see what you get: *If I set aside the grace of God, then Christ died in vain.*

This truth blew my mind. What was Paul teaching us here? He was saying that if we frustrate the grace of God, then Christ would have died in vain. If I frustrate the grace of God, then the death of Jesus would have been pointless. Do you see that? So, when I want to walk in the grace of God, I must remember Jesus' death.

What does this mean? It means that every time I say that something is impossible, I am nullifying Christ's death. If God says we can, and we say, "I don't think so," we are telling Him that Jesus died in vain and accomplished absolutely nothing. This form of rejecting God's Word is subtle because no one really stands up and opposes God. But if in character and behavior, you drag your feet or do anything contrary to what God declares about you, then you are saying, "No, I don't think so!" God is telling us that His grace is perfected through us as a result of Jesus' death, and His grace is just as intense and just as real as Jesus' death. Because Jesus died, no one can reverse the grace of God over our lives, and as much truth as lies in this statement, it is also true that we are the only ones who can walk away from the provision of His grace. This means that we can truly do all things through Christ, who strengthens us. It is all a result of His death.

As I was studying this truth, I saw a vision of a man trying to climb a steep hill. Then came someone else from behind to discourage him. He said to them, "Oh, please! I can do all things because Jesus died!" He continued to climb, but the other person said again, "You cannot do this!" He insisted, "Yes, I can. Jesus died! And that settles it." We can because He did what He did.

Being Stable

At first, Paul *"did not confer with flesh and blood"* **(Galatians 1:16).** Then, three years later, he went to Jerusalem to visit Peter for fifteen days (verse 18), but he did not see any of the other apostles. Other than that one visit, he *"was unknown by face unto the churches of Judaea which were in Christ"* **(verse 22).** They had not heard much about his activities, only that: *"he which persecuted us in times past now preacheth the faith which once he destroyed"* **(verse 23).** Their reaction to this was interesting: *"And they glorified God in me"* **(verse 24).**

There is a lot for us to study in chapter 2 of the book of Galatians, but we could summarize it in this way: After fourteen years, Paul finally returned to Jerusalem to confer with the other apostles. But why would he have insisted that he had not conferred with flesh and blood at first, and then that he had spent only fifteen days with Peter and did not see any of the others? It was so that God could get all the glory for what was happening in his life. He was not against relating to other people, only against allowing other people to negatively affect the grace of God that was working in his life.

Paul certainly did not isolate himself or act like he knew every-thing and refuse to deal with other people. He met Peter and stayed with him for fifteen days. After that, he went to other places and met other brothers. What is magnified here were his dealings with other men and women, which did not alter the message God had given him. Other people can sometimes derail you, but this grace of God has a way of keeping you on track; **grace will not permit you to be derailed**.

"So Soon Removed"

The teachings of the Book of Galatians were addressed to the Galatian Christians, and have much to say to us today. Early in the first chapter, Paul wrote:

I marvel that ye are so soon removed from Him that called you into the grace of Christ unto another gospel: which is not another; but there be some that trouble you, and would pervert the gospel of Christ. **Galatians 1:6-7**

The Galatians had the tendency of being swayed easily by the people around them, even to the point of turning back from the gospel that had saved them. Please think it not strange that this was happening; it would happen to anyone who is not firmly rooted in what they believe in. There must be a strong stance within every believer, the platform out of which all other teachings are tested and validated. The Galatians had been quickly "removed" from the life of grace and turned to "another gospel." How terrible! You and I cannot permit ourselves to be easily detached and extracted from the life of grace; such misfortune will prohibit us from entering, and even worse, experiencing the glorious future prepared for us in Christ Jesus.

How astonishing would it be if you had received God's grace and were walking in that grace, only to have someone come along and pluck you out of it? Paul was determined that it would not happen to him, and he wrote to the church of Galatia, admonishing them to erode such infiltration from their midst. He was not against relating with other people, but he was against allowing other people to adversely affect his life of grace. The grace of God must never be hindered, and it does not derail the one walking in it. How was Paul able to keep himself pure against the attempts of others to negatively influence him? Grace retained him; the grace of God does not derail.

In conclusion, one of the key components required to build a secure life is the ability to architecturally construct your life brick by brick. Patiently wait for each block to be solidified in its position before you place the next. In other words, start projects and see them through to the end. Many who fail to use this component become depressed and often give up when they realize there is nothing to show forth, after years and years of hard work. Remain consistent, for grace in itself does not derail; it is designed to retain its clients on their God-given path.

The Odd Man Out

Few of us like to stand out in a crowd, but when we walk in grace, we are usually the odd man out. Grace delivers a maturity that allows us to stand alone and stand tall, when others are compromising with the world around them. This same grace will also, for the same reason, enable us to rise and recover when we fall. Through grace, we can walk alone (if need be) or with kindred spirits. The grace of God does not derail. It leads us in the paths of righteousness for His name's sake. As long as we are in grace, we will not be derailed. Consequently, we have the responsibility of maintaining our covering and never allowing our grace to be derailed—it is our lifeline.

Walking in grace will take you far, even though you have to travel alone occasionally. You may even be considered unpopular, but know that you are doing great things through God's grace, and He is with you every step of the way. Attempting the road less traveled may not be fun, and often, you hear people say: "Well, everybody is doing it!" The fact that everybody is doing it doesn't mean that you should be doing it too. You can be the odd one in your class. You can be the odd one in your community. You can be the odd one in your family, and that is all right because one with God is majority.

Permit Yourself to Walk in Uniqueness

There is nothing wrong with individuality. To be unique is not a disease. To be unique is not a curse. **Our uniqueness is God's doing**. Each and every one of us has a unique set of fingerprints. We are created uniquely in every aspect. Others may see us as males and females, but we are not all the same in any sense of the word. There are vast differences between us. If God gives you children, they will not have your same fingerprints. Choose to be unique for God.

One day, while deliberating on some key challenges surrounding the need for difference and managing relationships, my wife said something so profound in explaining: "We do not have to fellowship with everyone. Being in a fellowship requires similar agenda. You must be a fellow in my ship if I have to fellowship with you." She added, "We must understand that not fellowshipping with someone does not necessarily mean you harbor a grudge against that individual."

Paul goes on to explain to us how to deal with individuals whose assignments or roles are different from ours. Everyone in your household can be going to one church, and you are going to another. All other members of your family could be physicians, but you are a lawyer. That's okay. Being different is okay. Being unique is okay. That assignment demands for us to stand out, and that is the reason for the difference and uniqueness. We ought to embrace variance, for God has given us the grace to walk in that unique nature.

Uniqueness Does Not Mean Perfection

Being unique does not mean that you are perfect, but the grace of God completes all things. If you are failing, trust in the grace of God that will remove you from the place of failure and move you into the position of success. Paul said it this way:

My strength is made perfect in weakness. **2 Corinthians 12:9**

If you happen to be unique in a bad way, walk in the grace of God so that He can promote you. He will pick you up from a state of bad things and bring you into a state of good things. Never celebrate or settle on an average state as ultimate because every state is but temporal until you exit the world's stage. Instead, say, "Lord, I thank You because I can make use of Your grace. I have failed so many times and hit rock bottom, so there is no place for me to go but up with Your grace." Then watch and see how the grace of God propels you into a place of victory. If you continue in the grace of God, you will never be moved either to the left or to the right. You will remain on course because the grace of God does not derail. If you do not continue in the grace of God, it is not His fault.

I have heard people accusing the anointing and accusing the grace of God for their failures, but the grace of God is perfect. If the grace of God is properly taught, sin, weakness, and shortcoming will flee. If the grace of God is properly communicated, failure is eliminated. If the grace of God is properly indoctrinated to Christians, then the House of God experiences strength beyond measure, because the omnipotence of God is made perfect in our weaknesses.

Determine to Stick with Grace

When Paul went to Jerusalem fourteen years after his conversion, he took Barnabas and Titus with him, and he said, *"I went up by revelation"* **(Galatians 2:1).** By that, he meant, his only motivation is the leading or nudging of the grace of God. He was alluding to the fact that walking in grace requires a deep insight into the workings and placements of things. The man was determined to stick to grace. He made sure his grace was fed, and he didn't let anybody influence it negatively.

No matter what people say or do, stick to your vision. Stick to your uniqueness. Stop trying to be someone else and end up as a cheap copy when you can be the original; build your own image. For some reason, I love to challenge those who have posters or large photos of famous people and celebrities on their walls. There is nothing wrong with celebrating greatness, but don't just celebrate the accomplishments of others. Do not fall into the intimidating position of thinking that other people are cut out for more, but hardly you. Make sure the success of others isn't the reason why you think too little of yourself. Determine to also be distinguished.

One day, while driving, I came upon a man operating a street sweeper, and I could see that he was thoroughly enjoying his work. That scene considerably marked and blessed me; indeed, the elements that produce joy are not external but rather internal. Therefore, whatever you do, passionately accomplish it well and be the best you can be. Whatever position you occupy in life, insist on enjoying it. The grace that is over your life is there so that you are not derailed. Lean on it!

Using Wisdom

Paul went on:

And I...communicated unto them that gospel which I preach among the Gentiles, but privately to them which were of reputation, lest by any means I should run, or had run, in vain. **Galatians 2:2**

What wisdom Paul had! He taught most people publicly, but he also taught others privately, and he had a reason for doing it:

"lest by any means I should run, or had run, in vain." He did not want anything to hinder or derail his work of grace. Interacting with other people is never an easy thing, and you and I must learn to do it well. Our goal in all interactions should be to bring forth fruitfulness or growth. Whatever you are doing, make sure you are doing it for the right reasons—to produce results for the advancement of the kingdom of God. As in the case of Paul, you will quickly notice that all human success and relationships are hardly about anything else but the proper managing of emotions. It is in this concept that lies adequate customer service mannerisms.

Most often, people tend to pay attention to what you have to say, only after seeing how much you genuinely care about them. Reach out to all, as though their only way out is you; put the Master's blood before you as a decent price for your deliberations. Remember His death and intentionally care for those you deal with as He—Jesus—would. May your love for the people you interact with leave them with lasting memories of goodwill, and above all, a glimpse of heaven and the Lord's unconditional love. Hopefully, when the Master looks down on your heart and actions, He smiles and says, "He did exactly what I would do."

A Matter of Protocol

Evidently, Paul was dealing with some people who preferred private ministry because of their reputations. They opted not to be seen in public with him. They were not hiding their faith but acting with discretion. The book of Romans declares that all "the powers that be are ordained of God" (Romans 13:1). When Paul met this type of people, he preached the gospel to them privately, leaving room for maturity, until they were able to handle and wisely merge this new experience. This was not a matter of pride, but a matter of protocol.

Some people seem to confuse the difference between being a secret disciple and wanting to hide the fact that they are a believer in Christ. Some say, "I don't want anyone to know that I have been born again." But when you become genuinely born again, you will want to let everyone know.

When you are truly born again, you will not have a problem with praying in public. You will not have a problem openly carrying your Bible. You will not hesitate to share your experience with others. Being ashamed of your state in Christ is what derails people's faith.

Resisting "False Brethren"

The phrase "false brethren" is used by Paul to describe people who are part of a club, group, association, or fold for a reason besides the belief system of the organization. Paul makes a point of the fact that Titus was a Greek, but that he did not allow anyone to force him to be circumcised. There were those who tried, and Paul called them "false brethren":

2And I went up by revelation, and communicated to them that gospel which I preach among the Gentiles, but privately to those who were of reputation, lest by any means I might run, or had run, in vain. 3Yet not even Titus who was with me, being a Greek, was compelled to be circumcised.

4And this occurred because of false brethren secretly brought in who came in by stealth to spy out our liberty which we have in Christ Jesus, that they might bring us into bondage. **Galatians 2:2-4**

These "false brethren" in Jerusalem were, in fact, genuine brothers who had deceptive motives in their dealings with Paul and the other believers. They projected one impression, but in reality, their intentions were very different. They were "false" because they pretended to be in agreement with Paul's doctrine. In actuality, they wanted to take Paul's converts and revert them back to legalism. Paul's emphasis is not that they were unsaved, but that they were "false" with him. Judas Iscariot was the type of disciple and club member who fellowshipped around the campfires of two opposing sides; he came around smiling and dining, yet had a secret agenda. Those who operate with dubious motives are "false" in the sense that they are feigning to be something they are not. This would qualify them in a certain sense as "false brethren."

Now, I want you to consider the phrase *"came in privily"* in Galatians 2:4, which describes how these false brethren behave. It originates from the Greek word *pareisago*. This word is a triple compound, comprised of the expression *para*, *eis*, and *ago*.

The word *para* means alongside. It denotes something that is very close, such as in the word *parasite*. The second part of the word, *eis*, means into and conveys the idea of penetration. Finally, the third part of this compound is the word *ago*. It just means "I lead."

When all these words are compounded together, *pareisago* ("came in privily") conveys the idea of smuggling something in undercover. Literally, it is a picture of someone who is leading (ago) something into (eis) the church, group, or an individual, alongside themselves (para). It is the idea of covert activity.

The first part of this compound—the word *para*—indicates that the deceptive motives of these false brethren are held so secretly that they are able to sneak right into the midst of the church or personal relationship undetected. By keeping their hidden agenda close to themselves, they are able to worm their way into positions of leadership. Once they gain ground inside a particular group, they start their destructive work from deep within the organization itself—Trojan horse tactic.

Paul was walking in grace, but these false brethren were still demanding allegiance to the law. They themselves had been derailed, and now they wanted to rob him and his followers of their liberty. Paul refused and fought their activities by reinstating the teachings of the truth of what they first believed. The same grace that had called him was now keeping him on track.

They had come to hear him, but he sensed that they really wanted to "spy out" the group's liberty, more like to see what made him tick. You might be so joyful in Jesus that someone comes to see you just to learn why you are smiling. Someone may want to know why you are so joyful when you wake up in the morning. What is it that you do differently? Do you brush your teeth differently? Someone will want to know. This is the reason the media of today loves to concentrate on other people's misery. No wonder, as the days go by, fewer and fewer people are willing to talk openly about their struggles and their successes.

When you talk about your struggles, people might say, "Hmm, really? If you have such struggles, then we can't be your friends anymore." But who doesn't have struggles? Be careful. Be on the lookout for people who just want to be your friend because of gain. They may have been sent to find out exactly what is making you smile, or what is making you tick. These may be people who just want the satisfaction of saying that they know you, that they know where you live, but then they may be much more dangerous.

In movies, we see secret agents coming to a man's house and asking his wife a series of questions with an agenda: "We want your husband. Help us catch him." The Bible shows us that some people are in our midst for the express purpose of bringing us back into bondage. We can't let that happen.

Let All Communicate Grace

Communication is such a big concept that has put even the very best in awkward situations at least once in their lifetime. It sounds simple, yet can present a very challenging and complex function. Communication goes beyond talking to someone; it is the effective transmission or exchange of information between individuals through a common system of symbols, signs, or behavior. This, therefore, requires an art if both parties involved, by any means, have to achieve their aim. This is where communication needs grace.

The Word teaches us that whatever we do, we should communicate grace to our hearers (Ephesians 4:29). Exchange nothing but grace. In other words, don't tell me that I have failed, but tell me how I can succeed. Don't point at only what I have been doing wrong. If all you do is run me down, I won't want to be around you. Show me the way out!

I need to be told that I can make it. I need someone who can take my hand and lead me to the next level. Don't just tell me my errors; tell me how I can improve upon them. Sometimes, when I ask people if they are willing to carry out their ideas, I have to insist, "If you are not prepared to carry out an idea, stop making idle statements into the air." For example, you are in a meeting, and someone asks you, "What can we do to improve things?" You answer in a derogatory manner, saying, "Well, I don't know, but maybe if you did this or did that..." "Maybe if you did?" Are you not part of the team? Why then exclude yourself from "we"? The moment you make a statement directed at other people, I know that you're not a builder, and I might not listen to you. Sarcasm never ministers grace.

Giving a Good Pep Talk

Some people call this a pep talk. During a challenging game, a coach will gather his players around him and encourage them. He tells them that he knows what they have inside of them and he knows that they can do better. He talks on and on in this way until those players are so hyped up that they get back in the game and win it. You and I must also know how to minister grace to our hearers.

As we grow in the Word and develop relationships, we must be careful to spend time with people who are not trying to pull us back into bondage. If I came to you, for example, and said that I was interested in getting into the nursing profession, don't immediately start talking about the problems with nursing. Don't tell me all the negative things you know that have happened to nurses. Have something constructive to say to me. Without constructive thoughts, there is something wrong with that kind of conversation. Carry out conversations with the intention of building rather than breaking, or else say nothing; in this way, you minister grace to the hearer.

If I come to you and tell you that I want to progress in any field, I should be able to see how to begin advancing from the advice you give me. You might say, "You know, I understand where you are coming from, but I think that if you take this route, it might be shorter for you," or "Have you done enough research on this? I believe there is a lot more that you might need to know." There is always a way to speak to someone so that what you have to say comes out positive rather than negative. We must understand this grace and realize it is not meant to derail the hearer.

They Laugh at Us

Most of us have been in that position in which we told someone that we wanted to venture in a particular direction, only to have them laugh and laugh. By the time they were done laughing, we felt like the most ridiculous person who ever lived. "Oh, so you want to be a preacher?" or "Oh, you want to get married, do you?" and they proceed to offer all sorts of negative comments. By the time they have finished, we feel like we are the only person on the planet who has ever made an error. If you did that to me, it would mean the end of our friendship. Friends should build each other up.

Use Constructive Criticism

Even when you are criticizing someone, it should be done in a constructive way. The Bible states: *"Blessed is the man that walketh not in the counsel of the ungodly, nor standeth in the way of sinners, nor sitteth in the seat of the scornful"* **(Psalm 1:1).** Contemptuous people laugh at you. They laugh at your misery. They also mock your success so that it looks like suffering. They say, "Well, you graduated. Now let's see how far you get in life." Personally, I would do everything in my power to go far, just because of such a statement. Don't let anybody push you down. Don't let anybody run you down. You have the grace not to be derailed.

Your True Friends

We learn in so many ways, often by the things that we come across in life. One such lesson came to me one day as I was looking into an investment tool that offered to send a letter that would help me explain investment opportunities to my friends. I noticed that when some people clicked on that menu and actually invested, I received an email stating: "This is to let you know who your real friends really are." I immediately wondered why they would put the message in those terms. I concluded that it was so that you could see that a friend was someone who wanted you to progress and wanted to progress with you, rather than bring you down.

When dealing with real friends, you often make statements like "Whatever you do, don't leave me behind" because you want to grow alongside them. "In your prayer meetings, don't leave me behind. In your Bible studies, don't leave me behind. In your progress, don't leave me behind. If you need to send me a text, by all means do. But, whatever you do, don't leave me behind." A friend who knows to be there when needed is a true friend and a reliable conduit of grace.

Paul Reacted Decisively

When the false brethren tried to find ways to rob Paul of his liberty in Christ, he acted very violently and with intent: *To whom we gave place by subjection, no, not for an hour; that the truth of the gospel might continue with you* **(Galatians 2:5).**

The Amplified Bible says it this way: *To them, we did not yield submission even for a moment, that the truth of the Gospel might continue to be [preserved] for you [in its purity].*

We must face such issues decisively. Know those with whom you talk on a regular basis. Know whose words matter in your life. Sometimes, after we have listened to other people talking, the purity of what we know inside of us, the conviction of what we are to be in life is shattered. Who do you listen to? Whose words matter to you? Determine, if possible by prayer, whose words are a law to you and whose words are meant to be discarded or minimized.

I have known so many confused people. Today they want to go into the Army. Yesterday it was the Navy. Tomorrow they will want

147

to be a firefighter or a nurse or an accountant. Their goals in life fluctuate with every new conversation or relationship.

This is bad. **The grace of God will bring you stability**. It will put continuity into your life and soul. It will keep you on track for prosperity.

Don't Allow Others to Darken Your Spirit

How can you prevent the messages of others from darkening your spirit? Don't listen to them—even for a moment! Have you noticed the key that is to be found in Galatians 2:5? It is the word *yield*. When you begin to listen to what someone is saying, it's like driving down a road and coming upon a YIELD sign. Someone has to yield. If, however, someone has come to you with bad intentions, refuse to yield. Their intention, whether they know it or not, is to completely derail you and keep you in bondage.

There is one thing that keeps people in bondage without fail every time; it is fear. The Word of God says: *"And deliver them who through fear of death were all their lifetime subject to bondage"* **(Hebrews 2:15).** Fear kept them in bondage "all their life, consequentially." How terrible! Refuse conversations and communications that transfer fear rather than faith, because such will keep you in bondage. Someone may say to you, "Oh no, you can't do that!" or they may ask, "Do you really think that God's hand is upon you for such and such?" Refrain from statements of fear, doubt, and unbelief; they will infiltrate your faith and drown your hope. As a person who desires to communicate grace to your hearers, when you notice someone around you has a certain talent, push them to develop it. If they drop their talent, you will have no reproach, but you would have done the right thing.

"God Accepteth No Man's Person"

Paul wrote:

But of these who seemed to be somewhat, (whatsoever they were, it maketh no matter to me: God accepteth no man's person:) for they who seemed to be somewhat in conference added nothing to me. **Galatians 2:6**

What did Paul mean by this? For example, if you were about to take on a major project, and a more endowed person walked in not to bring assistance but to scorn at the whole idea asserting themselves as being indispensible to you, then you will have to revert to the fact that no one is God and seek for ways to get the job done. Paul was not impressed with the apparent qualifications of others. If another person did not share his spiritual goals, he did not give them access or a place in his life. He was determined to stick with the grace of God.

This becomes all the more important when someone says to you, "You will not become anybody in this town unless and until I say so." That type of attitude tends to make us feel that we have been cursed. Paul refused to give place to such people, for he knew that *"God is no respecter of persons"* (Acts 10:34). So it doesn't matter who they are. God is not impressed, and so Paul was not moved either:

For they who seemed to be somewhat in conference added nothing to me: but contrariwise, when they saw that the gospel of the uncircumcision was committed unto me, as the gospel of the circumcision was unto Peter; (for he that wrought effectually in Peter to the apostleship of the circumcision, the same was mighty in me toward the Gentiles). **Galatians 2:6-8**

We must encourage our fellow man with statements like: "I can see the hand of the Lord upon you. God, who works in you, is doing great works. He is with you. That is clear to all. I can see that the blind are seeing, and the lame are walking." Know that God is with you too, and get to the place where you appreciate what He is doing in your life right now, as well as the lives of others. No need for competition, hatred, or any ill feelings. Small beginnings don't speak of failure at the end of any venture, but rather your starting point.

We serve a God of small beginnings. This is weaved in the working of the Kingdom of God as in a seed that eventually grows to be a great tree. The Word shows us that the Kingdom of God is like a seed. Whatever you do, even if it just starts as a tiny seed, hold on to it. After a while, it will become something entirely miraculous—a tree that can bear much fruit and also offer shelter (Matthew 13:31-32).

Acknowledging the Grace of God in Others

Now look at this passage:

And when James, Cephas, and John, who seemed to be pillars, perceived the grace that was given unto me, they gave to me and Barnabas the right hands of fellowship; that we should go unto the heathen, and they unto the circumcision. **Galatians 2:9**

This is where it all leads to: being able to acknowledge the grace of God in someone else's life. You should be able to say to them, "Move on, brother or sister." You should be able to tell them, "I recognize where you are going. Even though I am going in a different direction, we can still be friends and brothers." You should get to the point where you can say, "You go on and become an engineer. I have chosen to be a medical doctor. When I need help building my house, I'll come and see you. When you get sick, pay me a visit."

This kind of agreement is very powerful for anyone to achieve success. Someone put it this way: "Don't burn your bridges when you are moving forward." Another one said, "Take note of everyone you meet on your way up, because you might see them again on your way down." The friends who minister grace are those who associate with you and who will respond, when you have nothing and when you have plenty. Be such a friend yourself. Never become so big that your language changes or you can no longer sit with your associates. When you don't have a chair to sit on, I'll loan you one of mine.

There Must Be a Flow

The prophet Amos asked:

Can two walk together, except they be agreed? **Amos 3:3**

In order for two people to walk together, there must be a flow. When you recognize the grace of God that is in my life, make sure to give me the right hand of fellowship. Can you remember how Jonathan and David spoke to each other?

And it came to pass, when he had made an end of speaking unto Saul, that the soul of Jonathan was knit with the soul of David, and Jonathan loved him as his own soul. Then Jonathan and David made a covenant because he loved him as his own soul. And Jonathan stripped himself of the robe that was upon him and gave it to David, and his garments, even to his sword, and to his bow, and to his girdle. **1 Samuel 18:1 and 4-5**

That is what I'm talking about. Something in your spirit man should agree with your brother. Please take note that working together does not mean that we must all be of the same career or field of study. You mustn't all be engineers or physicians or preachers to come to a place of agreement. In a collaborative atmosphere or platform, the preacher can be the client of the physician while the physician is the client of the pastor without anyone undermining the other. The pastor should be free to lay lands on the medical doctor while the doctor is free to surgically work on the pastor or give him a prescription in case that comes up. We should be able to recognize the grace of God upon each other's lives and to extend the hand of fellowship.

Make Sure Your Flesh Does Not Interfere with What God Has Said

When we talk about the flesh, we are talking about the human part of us that is controlled by our soul. The soul is the seat of emotions—what we love, what we hate, what we prefer, what we are inclined to do or not do. These preferences are deep seated within every human being and are primordially the outcome of environment (upbringing) and impactful experiences (trauma). These likes and dislikes, or preferences, are the framework for all paradigms which lodge in our subconscious mind and filter our behavior.

Paul in Galatians 3:5 said "To them, we did not yield submission even for a moment, that the truth of the Gospel might continue to be [preserved] for you [in its purity], emphasizing here that he understands the place and influence of the flesh. Anyone who gives room to the flesh will be derailed from the path of the Lord because the flesh has no understanding or reverence for the things that pertain to the Spirit.

So you can see what Paul meant when he said, "I did not confer with flesh and blood." It is not flesh and blood that determines whether God speaks to me or not. This also means that whatever you do, you must make sure that your flesh does not interfere with what God has said. Such interference will alter the flow of grace.

Dealing with Ourselves

We have been speaking of the grace of God as it relates to dealing with other humans, but maybe we should take a few minutes to look at how to manage the grace of God when dealing with ourselves. To set the platform for this conversation, let us take into consideration this underlying reality: we are often our worst enemy.

This statement is true in so many ways. For instance, your cravings can be your enemies; they show up just when they know you will yield to them in the absence of external help. Your desires, your likes and dislikes, can be your enemies and they all reside within you. This enemy reveals itself in the things you say, for example: "This is how I want life to be; such a thing will never happen to me; I have had enough of this 'God said'; I feel like this, and I feel like that," all proceeding from the dictates of your soul. If some other person stood before you and made such statements, you probably would consider it ridiculous and you might feel like punching them—a thought that arises chiefly because you are not the one in the picture. (Maybe you should hit yourself every now and then, too, when you do or say the same things—sarcastically speaking.) The Bible teaches us:

For if we would judge ourselves, we should not be judged. **1 Corinthians 11:31**

Try to look under the surface of your life and discover the things that are crippling you and preventing you from achieving your goals. Your problem may not be "false brethren" who come to corrupt your thinking, a lack of resources, your environment, or a lack of powerful connections. It may just be your flesh or inner critic dictating, "You're too tired...pray tomorrow; that project is too big... you will probably fail; you are not that special; so-and-so is better placed than you..."

Please take the time to carefully analyze your world; take stock of the occurrences within you as well as the thoughts that orbit your mind. Notice the trends and patterns; notice the number of persons involved in the chatter. This exercise requires patience and self-control; you will get better with time. Make notes—write them down and face yourself as an informed expert. Now, do you still think the flesh, your thinking pattern, your inner critic are your friends in such moments as spiritual or mental upheaval? Is the flesh showing love and looking out for your future? Which do you think is more important to your future: prayer or sleep? And which does your flesh prefer? Please do not give your feelings the right hand of fellowship. Crucify them. Learn to tell your emotions, "It is Spirit time. You wait! When it is food time, then we'll talk about food."

It is so easy for us to point our fingers at other people, telling them what they need to deal with, but when it comes to dealing with personal matters, it becomes a major issue. Do whatever you need to do to get your flesh under control, because God is building us, preparing us to walk in something absolutely fantastic, and nothing must be allowed to hinder us.

This next point on how to deal with yourself when walking with grace is for people who are absolutely serious and desire to climb to the next phase of the journey. Seriousness is the prerequisite because at this point, you will need to deliberately and intentionally give up of your will by letting someone else have a say in your life. This is the phase that demands you to call the role of a mentor into your walk. A mentor is that person who understands you and will work with you until you become. He is not a friend in the sense of a playmate but a friend in that he is committed to your success, for therein lies his fulfillment. His words are law to you. These are things you must settle on if you will win with a mentor. We grow on the shoulders of others, and the experiences of a mentor are a time saver for your life and walk in grace. Make use of the experience!

(By the way, we are available to work with you should you need help. Please call the number at the end of the book or send us an email and someone will get back to you. I would love to personally work with you. We will start with 15 minutes of FREE consultation.)

Remember that Jesus Died

The death of our Lord and Savior Jesus Christ brought into view all things that pattern to life and godliness. A constant reminder of His death and resurrection keeps us on the redemptive plain, from which we glean on the inheritance He paid for with His blood, grace being of them. So, every time you want to walk in grace, remember the death of Jesus. The only way to avoid frustrating the grace of God is always to remember that He died to make it possible for you to walk in this grace. The death and resurrection of Jesus have given us immeasurable strength and access, and now we can say with the apostle Paul:

"I can do all things through Christ which strengtheneth me." **Philippians 4:13**

How does He strengthen us? For with the heart one believes, resulting in righteousness, and with the mouth confession is made, resulting in fusion with the Lord. This fusion brings out of us the benefits of the covenant relationship we have with the Lord, made possible by His death. Through our union with Christ, we are in-fused with divine ability. And, since nobody can revoke His death, then nobody can revoke His strength in us.

Therefore, I will go from one height to the next height because He has died, and nobody can change that fact. Behind this is the reason for the greatest battle ever waged against the advancement of the Kingdom of God—keeping the child of God and the world away from the truth. Several are, therefore, unaware that Jesus did die for them. But He died all right. He died, and He who died is the same who ascended that He may lead "captivity captive" (Psalm 68:18 and Ephesians 4:8). And now everything will be done according to His Word, not according to the culture of the day.

A Closing Prayer

In closing this chapter, I would like to stand in agreement with you for a shift in all that you set yourself to do, and also that you would encounter the grace of God in a whole new way. Please pray this prayer with me:

Let us start now by shouting out: Grace! Grace! to every mountain, every circumstance, and every challenge. Grace! Grace! Even to those things that are going well... We are in need for the new, the next, and the other.

Father,

I thank You for Your promise that Your grace will keep us stable. Your grace keeps us intact so that we will not stumble, neither will we fail.

Lord, thank You for the time and seasons in which we were on the ground; thank You that we were not knocked out but are still in Your grace.

I bless You, Father, that You have caused us to be established. You have caused us to be strengthened in Your grace. I ask that You would fill us to the brim with the knowledge of Your grace.

I appreciate You for showing us that You are our shepherd and that we will lack nothing. Lord, have Your way in our lives and pull us up to Your expectation. For Yours is the Kingdom, the power, and the glory.

I bless You, Father: To You be all the glory and all the honor.

In the name of Jesus,

Amen!

Fearlessness may be a gift but perhaps the more precious thing is the courage acquired through endeavor, courage that comes from cultivating the habit of refusing to let fear dictate one's actions, courage that could be described as "grace under pressure"—grace which is renewed repeatedly in the face of harsh, unremitting pressure.

Aung San Suu Kyi

CHAPTER 7

The Grace that Deflects

Before reading this next chapter, please pray with me:

Lord, I thank You for another opportunity to grow in Your grace. Refresh me, renew me, and lead me through in paths of righteousness for Your name's sake.

I declare that You are my shepherd, and I shall not want. I shall not lack any good thing. The lions may go hungry, but I shall lack no good thing. You are my shepherd. In You, I live; in You, I move; in You, I have my being.

In You dwelleth the fullness of the Godhead bodily, and I am complete in You. I am complete in the One who is the head of all principalities and all powers. In my faith, I am complete. In my joy, I am complete. I walk in favor, and I am complete. I walk in grace, and

I am complete. You are my Lord, and I am complete. You favor me, and I am complete. Favor is around me like a shield.

Thank you, Lord, for completing me,

In Jesus' name, Amen!

The Grace of God Deflects Evil

In this chapter, we will be looking at the ability of the grace of God to deflect. Before we dive in too quickly, a closer look at the word *deflect* will throw more light to the agenda of this chapter. To deflect means to cause something that is moving to change direction, either by hitting it and creating a sudden change in direction, or to keep something, such as a question, from affecting or being directed at a person or thing.

According to the Merriam-Webster Dictionary, In Latin, the word *flectere*, meaning "to bend" or "to curve," and its form *flexus* give us the roots *flect* and *flex*. Words from the Latin flectere have something to do with bending or curving. To flex is to cause something, such as a muscle, to curve or bend. Something flexible can be bent without breaking. To deflect, or turn aside, is to bend the direction of something.

Deflecting is used in sentences such as: armor that can deflect bullets, or the goalie deflected the ball with his hands. Also in politics in statements like: They are trying to deflect attention from the troubled economy, or the blame was deflected from the chairman.

The Grace that Deflects

So when talking about the grace that deflects, I am saying that everything that is set on a course to put you down, kill you, paralyze you, etc. will be hit and forced to change direction. Meaning, whatever thing may come your way, you will not be affected adversely. No weapon formed against you shall prosper. The grace of God deflects it. The point here is not that there will be no enemy or challenges, but that whatever artillery is devised against you will ultimately fail. There will be plagues, but nothing shall by any means hurt us. At the beginning of the chapter, I mentioned that the favor of God encompasses us like a shield. You might know His grace to represent goodness, mercy, and favor and yet the expressions of grace bring about shield-like abilities as well.

He said in His Word:

"For thou, Lord, wilt bless the righteous; with favor wilt thou compass him as with a shield." **Psalm 5:12**

Whoso keepeth the commandment shall feel no evil thing: and a wise man's heart discerneth both time and judgment. **Ecclesiastes 8:5**

In other words, when things come against us, His grace deflects them.

Yea, though I walk through the valley of the shadow of death, I will fear no evil: for thou art with me; thy rod and thy staff they comfort me. **Psalm 23:4**

The psalmist could say this because the grace of God was deflecting all evil.

Cast Off Pride

The Lord is my shepherd, so I shall not want. Shepherds take care of sheep, although they may be responsible for goats as well. They must be on call for their animals around the clock because you can never tell what will happen in the course of the day. A shepherd's primary responsibility is the safety and welfare of the flock; he will graze the animals, herding them to areas of healthy food and keeping a watchful eye out for poisonous plants. He makes sure we are blessed going out and blessed coming in. He dresses the lilies and feeds the birds, so He can and will take care of us. Our covenant relationship with the Good Shepherd demands that we trust and have faith in Him and His ability to show up for us, in ways we cannot even initiate. It is time then, to stop complaining, murmuring, and worrying, which are all offspring of pride and unbelief. Let faith lift you up.

What is pride? Pride is the characteristic that a person exhibits when they have lost consciousness of the promises of the Word of God. It is when such a person begins to see his knowledge of things as being superior to that of the Master: God. This air of superiority gives a false impression of perfection that blinds an individual from seeing the loopholes and pitfalls every one of us naturally has all around. Therefore, pride will precede a fall; it will cause you to get off the rails of grace and into the wisdom of the world. The sagacity of the world is earthly, unspiritual, and demonic. For wherever jealousy and selfish ambition exist, there you will also find disorder and evil of every kind. But the wisdom from above is first of all pure. It is also peace-loving, gentle at all times, and willing to yield to others. It is full of mercy and good deeds. It shows no favoritism and is always sincere. The spirit of pride will cause you to lose consciousness of the Lord Jesus Christ, and eventually, God Himself.

Young men, in the same way, submit yourselves to your elders. And all of you, clothe yourselves with humility toward one another, because, "God opposes the proud, but gives grace to the humble." **1 Peter 5:5**

A man's pride will bring him low, But a humble spirit will obtain honor. **Proverbs 29:23**

Dear friends, post the following prayer at all the junctions on your path: bathrooms, kitchen, car, bedside wall, etc. Repeat it as often as you possibly can, understanding that its words will create out of you the best in Jesus' name.

I shall lead with my ears, follow up with my tongue, and let anger straggle along in the rear. God's grace doesn't grow from human violence or passion. So I throw all spoiled virtue and cancerous evil in the garbage. In simple humility, I let my gardener, God, landscape me with the Word, making a salvation-garden of my life. I receive with a gentle spirit the wisdom from above, and I shall experience salvation. This I declare in Jesus' name, Amen!

Rest in Grace

Paul was amazed that the Galatians were removed so easily from their walk of grace. When the Lord is your shepherd, you are not easily removed or derailed. The Word of God promises:

He leadeth me beside the still waters. **Psalm 23:2**

Meaning that God is not the author of storms, and He prepares no evil experience for His children; therefore, it is not our portion to be troubled because our boat is tossed to and fro. Paul did experience shipwreck, and Jesus' boat took in water because of the storm, but He was in perfect peace in the midst of it all. Our platform may be going through an earthquake, or our environment overhauled by chaos, but we will have peace in the midst of it.

Thou wilt keep him in perfect peace, whose mind is stayed on thee: because he trusteth in thee. **Isa 26:3**

That is the reason God advises us not to be troubled by what is happening around us. He has overcome. He has scheduled peace for you and me.

Those who love Your law have great peace, And nothing causes them to stumble. **Psalm 119:165**

Peace I leave with you, my peace I give unto you: not as the world giveth, give I unto you. Let not your heart be troubled, neither let it be afraid. **John 14:27**

The Lord is our shepherd, so we shall not want. He completes us and brings into our lives such things as are necessary and on time too. As a result, God could tell His servants that they did not need to fight, for He would fight for them. Please understand this truth: regardless of what we are ever going to deal with, our enemy is not physical, and therefore our warfare is not carnal, but mighty through God. Waging war in the spirit requires this understanding so we can permit the Lord, who is Spirit, to fight as He promised. So, my friend, you do not need to fight in this battle; station yourselves, stand, and see the salvation of the LORD on your behalf. Do not fear or be dismayed; tomorrow, get out there and face the trials and challenges, for the LORD is with you. The LORD will fight for you; you need only to be still. Your Father wants to stand for you. He wants to take your place, even as Jesus Christ did while on the cross. His agenda didn't start today, and it is not just a suggestion for the future. Our Lord has been doing it all along:

While we were yet sinners, Christ died for us. **Romans 5:8**

Permit Him to do what He knows to do BEST!

Growing in the Grace of God

Oh, how blessed we are with such a marvelous grace. What more to do but to seek more, be more, have more, and do more. Growing and tactically walking in the mysteries provided us is of paramount importance. Let us continue to look at examples of how we can increase in grace. All of us should be growing in this grace. I am believing the Lord, that by the time you finish reading this book, you will stop seeing impossibilities and stop living in guilt. Guilt is not of God. There is no place in the Bible in which we are admonished to live with a guilty conscience. We can experience something that the Bible calls "godly sorrow":

For godly sorrow worketh repentance to salvation not to be repented of: but the sorrow of the world worketh death. **2 Corinthians 7:10**

Godly sorrow brings us to repentance, and that leads to salvation. Therefore, godly sorrow leaves us cleansed of all unrighteousness with no guilt. If you have never experienced godly sorrow, then you cannot repent. Clearly, in that lies the difference between guilt and godly sorrow. Guilt says, "Oh, my goodness, I can't believe I did that." yet produces no change. Godly sorrow says, "This is not what I want. Oh, Lord, help me! How did I find myself here? Please, Lord, help me find my way back to You."

Godly sorrow causes us to repent, but guilt leaves us in emotional limbo. Godly sorrow ushers in grace and the will to rise and forge forward, but guilt ushers in the sense of defeat and the desire to quit. Guilt magnifies the fallen individual and their weakness and removes the consciousness of God from the picture. Many people backslide and remain in that state because of the guilt they feel when they have failed in some way.

Again, the foundation for a guilty conscience is pride, and pride is the thing that happens to you when your focus becomes self or the ego, and not God. Have you ever been in a place where you say, "Look at what that person did to me?" Such a statement is the result of pride, especially when you make it from a place of scorn or belittling. The truth here is that anyone can make errors. If it were different in that you were the one who did wrong—any kind of wrong—your statement would be more like, "I can't believe I did this to the Lord." As a general phenomenon, when people do wrong, they expect mercy and a second chance, yet come down hard on someone else when they do wrong. Cast your cares upon the Lord, and let Him carry all your heavy burdens. Release grace to others as you would expect grace to be shown to you.

The Grace to Transform

In sports, we train those who will act as a defense because we want to deflect all shots from an opposing team. Firefighters wear special suits to deflect the heat of the fire. Police officers wear bulletproof vests to deflect potential bullets. Deflection can stop a bullet or even send it back with equal or lesser force. You see, His angels shall bear you up, and you shall not dash your foot against a stone. Scripture does not speak of the absence of the stone, but the protection provided against the rock. The grace of God we are talking about is the supernatural ability that God employs to shield us. Again, the psalmist wrote:

For thou, Lord, wilt bless the righteous; with favor wilt thou compass him as with a shield. **Psalm 5:12**

The above scripture describes the presence of grace, manifesting as favor, wrapped all around us. Take a moment to visualize a shield covering every part of your stature; literally, every part enclosed. One of the things that people around you will notice about the transformation in your life is that you now face adversity differently. If someone decides to pick a fight with you, you no longer respond as you once would have. The grace of God that deflects has taken over your being in such a way that every negative word uttered against you naturally falls to the ground and does not inflame you as before. If you open up even more, you will notice a tremendous growth of peace within you leading to more deflection of negativity.

Like Jesus, it will be said of you: Like a sheep to slaughter, and so much thrown at him, he did not open his mouth to say a thing. Even

169

now, begin to picture sickness, accusations, betrayal, and scandal deflected from you, your loved ones, or people you touch with your prayers. Visualize rage coming towards you like a storm, and also see it dying out like the waves of the sea. Desire this and cultivate it in your life. We grow in grace as we grow in knowledge. Accept it as your new normal. Jesus died to ensure such tranquility. He has already overcome. May your life suddenly shift from now on in Jesus' name, Amen!

The Twofold Purpose

This teaching has a twofold purpose:

The **first** is for those who have already experienced the grace of God that deflects. My prayer for you is that you will grow in that grace.

The **second** is for those who once experienced it, but lost it. My prayer for you is that you will consciously walk in it again.

The grace that deflects has been made available unto all men. It is up to you to walk in the daily awareness of that grace. Sometimes, when negative things creep into our thoughts, and we meditate on them, they get into our spirits. If we continue to meditate on them, then we are willfully choosing to neglect the grace of God. Decide to disagree with such thoughts, and you will see the grace of God reactivated in that area of your life. But you must make a conscious decision to do this.

Do Not Neglect God's Grace

The Word of God cautions us against ignoring the grace of God. Do the opposite. Stir it up. Right now, as you are reading this book, the words within its pages are reviving the grace that deflects in your spirit. Grace is provided to deflect everything negative that has taken root in you. Such things have a way of keeping your mind away from the Deflector (our God). So the more of the Word of this book you take in, the more that thing will lose its grip over you. The Bible states emphatically,

Faith cometh by hearing, and hearing by the word of God. **Romans 10:17**

So we could say deflection comes by hearing and hearing more of the Word of God. Permit the constant assimilation of the Word of God to create for you a holy-fortified grill suited to deflect from you all and anything that does not align with God's purpose for you.

Activated Grace Through Praise

Praise is more than just singing. It is a declaration of faith; a proclamation of God's victory over past, present, and future battles. It is an affirmation of who the authentic King is. Anyone who, therefore, indulges in praises will without fail experience praise as a weapon. While Paul and Silas were doing the work of God in Philippi, they were arrested and taken to jail. Neither of them complained that God was not protecting them. They didn't question God about where their miracle was. Instead, they began to activate the grace that deflects through praise and worship.

You see, when you praise and worship, you enter a numbing realm in which there is no pain or sorrow. In this realm, your senses are disconnected from your state of affairs and fixed on the Majesty. You are physically here on Earth but spiritually present with the Father. It is a moment of bliss which reveals grace. While Paul and Silas were praising and worshipping, the Holy Ghost showed up, the jail was shaken open, and they were set free. According to Zechariah 4:7, whenever we sing praises to God, we are shouting "Grace! Grace!" within the words and expressions.

Someone might ask, "How can you shout, 'Grace! Grace!' when there is a mountain in front of you?" The answer is by faith! By letting go of the control and the "figuring out," you permit yourself to enter that place of trust. You cannot do this by your power; you will have to let go and let God. You can shout because this grace deflects any negative thing that is thrown at you. God has promised in His Word that He will make that mountain become level ground.

Paul and Silas prayed and sang praises despite the fact that they had been beaten and injured. They were not focusing on their pain, but on God, and grace was stirred up within them. When that grace was sufficiently stirred up, their chains fell off, and the prison could no longer hold them. That is what happens when we praise the Lord. Circumstances can be so challenging that we experience much pain and stress and so tormenting that our bodies reach their breaking point. Nevertheless, know this: miracles will happen in an atmosphere of praise and will stretch out to others in similar situations.

The Grace of God Changes Your Reactions

This grace deflects anger. It deflects negative utterances and actions that otherwise might erupt into major disasters. In the account of Paul and Silas' ordeal, in which they were jailed without any just cause, not only did the grace of God deflect their pain but it also enabled them to walk in joy all the way to the jailor's house. While at the jailor's house, they led his family to the Lord, and after that, they permitted their new friends to attend to their wounds. Isn't that just amazing? There was no negative impact on them, but rather a praise report. There was no negative attitude, no blaming of God, no expressing of anger or praying thunderous prayers against those who jailed them.

They were far from messing things up with their reactions (negative feedback or kickback—doing something on account of someone else's actions) but rather they acted out grace. They preached the gospel to them and entered the water to baptize those new believers (Acts 16:33). How do you react when you hear bad news? If you don't apply the grace of God that deflects, bad news can overcome you or drown you with sorrow. When you see or hear something harmful or damaging, don't panic. At that moment, step into grace, and by faith, push back the darkness. Take control of the reins and manifest complete confidence, for Jesus is not just the Way but also Master of the wheel.

Carry out these actions with this simple prayer:

Thank you, Lord, for this opportunity through which I shall experience You at another level. I step into grace right now in the name of Jesus. Lord Jesus, take the wheel. You are keeping me in perfect peace right now because my mind is focused on You.

You and I win always. Now I move forward toward the testimony because a good report awaits me.

Thank You, Lord.

In Jesus' name,

Amen.

Following these directions will transport you in a direction opposite of fear. Use this as a picture and reflection of complete rest; a perfect example of that place of faith in God.

Without Grace, There Is Chaos

The opposite of faith, rest, or confidence is chaos. The Bible admonishes us to begin:

...building up yourselves on your most holy faith, praying in the Holy Ghost
Jude 1:20

Your most holy faith, the perfect place of rest, is the place where your emotions are no longer involved. When your emotions are no longer involved, you are in a place of perfect faith, and the result is perfect peace. The clothes we wear or houses we dwell in never reveal a person's true nature, but rather how they react under pressure. Things happen, and with each experience, though we may not understand why or what benefits we procure, we each should be able to take the positive from every experience and use it to minister to others.

God never promised peace in this external world. He rather prophesied chaos; wars and rumors of wars, father against son, a daughter against her mother, sword between siblings, imprisonment for disciples, etc., yet the child of God shall dwell in peace in their being; not in isolation but in peace within the chaos—totally immovable.

Never Fast and Pray Out of Fear

Stepping into grace means moving into peace. Faith is the symbol of tranquility. As children of grace, we never fast and pray out of fear of the unknown. When you fast and pray, do it in faith. Build yourself up on your most holy faith. Never tear yourself down through fear. Paul wrote:

We are troubled on every side, yet not distressed; we are perplexed, but not in despair; persecuted, but not forsaken; cast down, but not destroyed.
2 Corinthians 4:8-9

This scripture vividly demonstrates the power and thorough work of the grace that deflects. This grace keeps us from distress and counters every potential stress of life.

Saved in the Midst of Your Battles

In the life of David, he credits the victories from battles to the Lord. In his writings, he utters declarations that originated from his personal experiences on battlefields, as well as day-to-day plots over his life. One of these statements is:

A thousand shall fall at thy side, and ten thousand at thy right hand; but it shall not come nigh thee. There shall no evil befall thee, neither shall any plague come nigh thy dwelling. **Psalm 91:7, 10**

David – The Name on Everyone's Lips

Similar to the earth that produces pleasant and unpleasant crops, when your name is on everyone's lips such as on TV and "testimony land," you get to have praises and battles you never anticipated. Such was the case when the soldiers returned home, after David had defeated the Philistines; the women poured out of all the villages of Israel singing and dancing, welcoming King Saul with tambourines, festive songs, and flutes. In playful frolic, the women sang, "Saul kills by the thousand, David by the ten thousand!"

This type of parade is not a favorable thing, especially if you have a leader who loves the praises of men, and if you are the sort of person who also relishes recognition. As was the case with David, this mode of singing and the words used made Saul angry—very angry. He took it as a personal insult. He said, "They credit David with 'ten thousand' and me with only 'thousands.' Before you know it they'll be giving him the kingdom!" From that moment on, Saul kept his eye on David.

Landing Strip

A landing strip is a long, flat area of ground that is used by aircrafts when taking off and landing. With this definition in mind, the intention of this section is to make sure that we are working with the grace that deflects, and not making provision for the devil's aircraft to land, thereby falling prey to his assaults.

The Lord Jesus anticipated a series of events, leading up to but not limited to His crucifixion. In the course of one of the meetings with His disciples, in which He discussed many of these things, He made one of the most powerful statements ever:

Hereafter I will not talk much with you: for the prince of this world cometh, and hath nothing in me. **John 14:30**

In the Amplified version, it reads, *"The ruler of the world (Satan) is coming. And he has no claim on Me."* Jesus was saying here that, though He is the Son of God, He had to make sure that Satan has no basis for a claim on Him. Our statutory relationship with God does not prohibit Satan from laying a claim over us. A perfect example will be in the case of Satan laying claims over the body of Moses the man of God, outlined in the book of Jude. Jesus was saying, make sure you have no "landing strip" for the devil. "[He has nothing in common with Me; there is nothing in Me that belongs to him, and he has no power over Me.]"

Three things we can identify as lessons here:

Firstly, battles mostly occur in the absence of your mentor or leader; they happen when you are alone, especially mentally. They happen when you lose consciousness of the principles that lead your life.

Secondly, if there is something in you that belongs to Satan, you will lose the battle, because both of you would look the same, and that gives him authority over you.

Thirdly, all battles are primarily won internally, and not externally. Our internal dialogue determines our successes and failures. We manifest externally what our world is internally—an exact mirror reflection.

As one would expect from the above explanation, the next day an ugly mood was sent to afflict Saul, who became quite beside himself, raving. David played his harp, as he usually did at such times to help alleviate the occurrence. Saul, who at the time had a spear in his hand, suddenly threw the spear, thinking, *I'll nail David to the wall*. David ducked, and the spear missed. This happened twice.

This occurrence made Saul, an experienced warrior, to fear David greatly. It was clear that God was with David and had left Saul. So, Saul got David out of his sight by making him an officer in the army. David was in combat frequently. Everything David did turned out well. Yes, God was with him. For Saul, seeing David become more successful caused him to grow more fearful because he could see the handwriting on the wall; power had changed hands. But everyone else in Israel and Judah loved David. They loved watching him in action. These instances are all the work of the grace that deflects in his life. Proving more and more that the grace that does not derail in collaboration with the grace that deflects were working together to keep David on the path to greatness, as promised by the Lord. The grace that deflects kept David in battles and all sorts of diabolical schemes.

Discern the Spirit at Work

The grace that deflects, in collaboration with the spirit of discernment. The Lord is the one who orders the steps of the righteous, and you and I need to not only be aware of this, but delve into it for its tremendous benefits. One day Saul said to David, "Here is Merab, my eldest daughter. I want to give her to you as your wife. Be brave and bold for my sake. Fight God's battles!" But all the time Saul was thinking, *The Philistines will kill him for me. I won't have to lift a hand against him.* David, embarrassed, answered, "Do you really mean that? I'm from a family of nobodies! I can't be son-in-law to the king." The wedding day was set, but as the time neared for Merab and David to be married, Saul reneged and married his daughter off to Adriel the Meholathite. Meanwhile, Saul's daughter Michal was in love with David.

When Saul was told of this, he rubbed his hands in anticipation. "Ah, a second chance. I'll use Michal as bait to get David out where the Philistines will make short work of him." So again he said to David, "You're going to be my son-in-law." Saul ordered his servants, "Get David off by himself and tell him, 'The king is very taken with you, and everyone at court loves you. Go ahead, become the king's son-in-law!'" The king's servants told all this to David, but David held back. "What are you thinking of? I can't do that. I'm a nobody; I have nothing to offer."

When the servants reported David's response to Saul, he told them to tell David this: "The king isn't expecting any money from you; only this: Go kill a hundred Philistines and bring evidence of your vengeance on the king's behalf. Avenge the king on his enemies." (Saul expected David to be killed in action.) On receiving this message, David was pleased. There was something he could do for the king that would qualify him to be his son-in-law! He lost no time but went right out, he and his men, killed the hundred Philistines, brought their evidence back in a sack, and counted it out before the king—mission completed! Saul gave Michal, his daughter, to David in marriage.

As Saul more and more realized that God was with David, and how much his own daughter, Michal, loved him, his fear of David increased and settled into hate. Saul hated David. Whenever the Philistine warlords came out to battle, David was there to meet them—and beat them, upstaging Saul's men. David's name was on everyone's lips.

You, too, will be saved in the midst of your battles, as you open up to the grace of God that deflects every evil. No evil will come near your dwelling.

Flourishing Like a Palm Tree

Paul was accustomed to trouble, and understood that the Lord would always get him out of it, but he also knew that the devil could thwart his assignment in some ways. So he cautioned believers not to be ignorant of the devices of the enemy. Pitfalls do not automatically disappear because we are unaware of their presence. Those who know their God shall be strong and do exploits. The promise of salvation is only completed because it includes prosperity. Not only shall we be saved, but we shall be established in and by the grace of God.

The righteous shall flourish like the palm tree. **Psalm 92:12**

The palm is flexible and, as a result, possesses the ability to bounce back. When the wind goes against the palm tree, it bends over in the direction of the wind. It seems to stretch, at times, down to the ground, but to its flexible nature, it always comes back standing up tall. You and I are like the palm tree. Even if we are cut on or partially buried, just like the palm tree, we will still produce.

Bearing the Death of Jesus

Paul continued his teaching to the Corinthians as he taught them the importance of *always bearing about in the body the dying of the Lord Jesus, that the life also of Jesus might be made manifest in our body. For we which live are always delivered unto death for Jesus' sake, that the life also of Jesus might be made manifest in our mortal flesh* (**2 Corinthians 4:10-11**).

If you keep bearing about as in owning the death of Jesus, then the life of Jesus will also manifest in your body, and this will propel you to where—regardless of what people say or whatever the devil throws at you—you shall emerge victoriously. Press on then, using the example of Jesus:

He was oppressed, and he was afflicted, yet he opened not His mouth: He, brought as a lamb to the slaughter, and as a sheep, before her shearers is dumb, so he openeth not his mouth **(Isaiah 53:7).**

Speak to Your Mouth

Out of the mouth of babes and sucklings has He ordained strength. And we are told that death and life are in the power of the tongue. The tongue yields its benefits—the creation of death and/or life to those who love it. We need to shut our mouths and only talk when absolutely necessary. If you have a problem in this regard, kindly consider that God has given you authority over all the works of His hands including the tongue.

Therefore, you can speak to your mouth and command it to say just what the Spirit of God wants it to say. You can command it to glorify God at all times. As you indulge in domesticating your tongue, you must understand you can only go as far as the Lord determines. Renewing your language is not done by power or might. Make the training of your tongue a prayer topic, and let God miraculously take over your tongue and make His words yours. The benefits shall be the communication of grace to your hearers. May this be your portion in Jesus' name, Amen!

All "for Jesus' Sake"

In that 11th verse, Paul shows that it was all for Jesus' sake:

For we which live are always delivered unto death for Jesus' sake, that the life also of Jesus might be made manifest in our mortal flesh. **2 Corinthians 4:11**

If something happens to us because of Jesus, then it is a regular part of the Christian life. In the early years of my own Christian experience, I would reflect on the persecutions I was facing and thank God just for being alive. The result was that others came to Christ through my testimonies. There is triumph for you as well as for others in all instances of persecution.

Made of Some Strong Stuff

Again, Paul wrote: *"We are troubled on every side, yet not distressed."* We are made up of some adamant strong stuff. When anything negative comes our way, the grace that deflects puts it down. Therefore, we can take the scriptural promises seriously:

I shall not die, but live, and declare the works of the Lord. **Psalm 118:17**

Stick with and grow in the grace of God, and you will be victorious. Your fabric is not made with fiber that was picked up from the roadside; this strong stuff is the merchandise of God—the grace that deflects.

Speak Faith

When we talk about speaking from a place of faith and speaking faith, we are not just talking about speaking positively. Positive speaking and positive thinking are controlled by the five senses, but speaking faith proceeds from an altered tongue influenced by a faith-filled spirit.

Faith—the assurance that God will come through—is a spiritual commodity and requires hearing and hearing the Word of God. The Word of God contains the words used by the Almighty God to equip this world with everything in it. You will be doing yourself a favor when you fill your consciousness with these words. You, too, will be well on your way to creating the kind of world you desire by using the creative words God used.

When one is in faith, one is influenced to speak positively because faith is already positive. On the other hand, you can speak positively and not be in faith. Remember that faith comes by hearing and hearing by the Word of God. Faith is beyond courage or the bold stand we take in the face of a challenge. Positive thinking is just that, thinking positively. Faith speaking comes from hearing faith-filled words; the constant hearing of the possibilities of God in the lives of others has a way of telling you that all things are possible for the one who believes.

When we are speaking the language of faith, we call those things that be not as though they were thereby calling nonexistent things into existence. We bring to the scene whatever we say, so why not say what we would want to see. It is the same breath and the same energy used to create evil as is used to create good. Stick to the good.

The Word of God is assuring; it is creative and has the tendency of emboldening the hearer into thinking as big as God would. Speaking the language of faith is a call to walk the hall of fame of those who had gone before you, stepping into their shoes and conforming their stories to your current life.

Like a prayer, you will begin to speak into your life and give direction on things that you never saw breaking forth. This experience will cause you to see things that are not present in the natural. You will begin to dream and write down the experience. The realm of possibilities will be open to you and creativity will begin to flow out of you. Everything you now see and deal with will be viewed from the place of vision and assurance. You now know you are not alone—God is with you, and this deep inner knowing paves all you say. You now speak faith.

Faith is the substance of things hoped for, the evidence of what we do not see. It is the product of hearing the Word of God over and over. To move in faith, we need to know what the Word of God says regarding the situation or condition upon which we desire to employ faith. Therefore, faith is activated when the will of God is known. Faith not only demonstrates the mind of God, but also transforms its possessor's language. Faith further enables the child of God to be a conduit of the will of God. As a result, whatever we communicate has to be in alignment with God's will. As it is written,

I believed, therefore have I spoken. **Psalm 116:10**

Since we have that same spirit of faith, we also believe and, therefore, speak. **2 Corinthians 4:13**

Whatever situation you find yourself in, do not be silent. Speak from a place of faith to keep the grace of God activated, and let that grace of God deflect everything that needs diverting. Clearly, a closed mouth puts a cap on your destiny and leaves your life without flavor, and if you speak the wrong things, you will speak your way into your death.

The Advantage Mindset

Please, permit me to use someone who is not necessarily a biblical character to drive this point across. Confucius once said, "The one who says he can and the one who says he cannot are both right." Doing things in a certain way is the one singular thing that will make a huge difference in your type of results, as is expected or unexpected, and the quantity of return you get. When you face things from the platform of already being defeated, then based on probability, you are defeated; but if you face life from the standpoint of success, then chances are you will experience a positive outcome.

I encourage you to have all-night prayers, mission ventures, raising the dead, etc., but do so from a place of victory and not out of weakness or defeat. Do whatever you are doing out of the strength of God and not the totality of your shortcomings; for the joy of the Lord is your strength. Always be in a rejoicing mode because you know the answer has already come. God's grace is at work in your life.

"Troubled on Every Side"

Paul wrote: *Great is my boldness of speech toward you, great is my glorying of you: I am filled with comfort, I am exceeding joyful in all our tribulation. For, when we were come into Macedonia, our flesh had no rest, but we were troubled on every side; without were fightings, within were fears. Nevertheless God, that comforteth those that are cast down, comforted us by the coming of Titus; and not by his coming only, but by the consolation wherewith he was comforted in you, when he told us your earnest desire, your mourning, your fervent mind toward me; so that I rejoiced the more* **(2 Corinthians 7:4-7).**

With this in mind, he arrived at this conclusion:

For which cause we faint not; but though our outward man perish, yet the inward man is renewed day by day. **2 Corinthians 4:16**

Thank God for Titus. He was able to minister some much-needed grace to Paul. Make sure that when you speak, you minister gracefully and also transfer the same grace to your hearers, even as Titus demonstrated. I encourage you to keep CDs and tapes of the Word of God and good preaching of the Word of God in your homes and cars so that you can continuously listen to them and build yourself up in your most holy faith. Let grace work in you, and then minister grace to others.

Pray with me now in closing this chapter:

Lord,

We thank You that our lives will never be the same because of the grace that deflects. We roll every burden and care onto You. We declare that we are worry-free, complaint-free people. We will not murmur, and we will not complain. Instead, we will proclaim, "Grace! Grace!"

In Jesus' name! Amen!

"Timing is so important! If you are going to be successful in dance, you must be able to respond to rhythm and timing. It's the same in the Spirit. People who don't understand God's timing can become spiritually spastic, trying to make the right things happen at the wrong time. They don't get His rhythm—and everyone can tell they are out of step. They birth things prematurely, threatening the very lives of their God-given dreams."

— T. D. Jakes

CHAPTER 8

The Timing of God's Grace

As we explore this section, I would like to put forth a foundation for this concept. The idea of timing with grace is somewhat ludicrous, especially when we consider the misconception some have of grace to mean disorderliness. Please, understand that grace is not an isolated notion operating outside the confines of all other scriptural concepts. There is such a thing as a time, a crack in the wall, a door of opportunity in the functioning and operations of grace. The timing of grace is a compilation of the sovereignty of God and the obedience exhibited by the child of God. Jesus lamented over Jerusalem because they were not aware of the hour of their visitation. God was ready to move, but they were not in a position to welcome His move. The time of visitation is the time to favor Zion. So, herein lies the controversy and the challenge: The sovereign God desires to take us places, but for this to happen, we need to be in agreement with Him. Pray with me before we begin the study.

Let Us Pray

Father,

In the name of Jesus, I thank You for Your grace upon my life, and even now, I shout, "Grace! Grace!" Indeed, this mountain is becoming a plain before me, in the name of Jesus. It is not by might and not by power, but by the Spirit of the Lord.

I acknowledge and declare: The shout of the King is with me, and no enchantment or divination will work against me. I will prosper, live on, and do well, all because of Your grace.

Thank You for Your grace so that I can declare: "The Lord is my shepherd. I shall not want. You have said unto me, 'Do not be afraid,' and 'I will never leave you, I will never forsake you,' so that I may boldly say, 'You are my Helper. I shall not be afraid of what man can do unto me.'"

I am Your beloved. You keep me, and You shield me. Under Your wings do I trust. Surely goodness and mercy shall follow me all the days of my life because of Your grace.

In Jesus' name,

Amen!

Some People the Lord Wanted Me to Meet

While driving one day, on my way to a meeting, I was instructed by God to take a particular exit because there were some people He wanted me to meet. As I followed the leading upon my heart, I felt a pull to stop at an acquaintance's home. Once I got there, I met two ladies. One of them was a Jehovah's Witness, and the other was Roman Catholic. A conversation developed that led us to talk about the subject of grace. In fact, as I began to speak about the grace of God, you can imagine the rest of the story. Those two ladies became so intrigued with the concept that a revival broke out right there.

It was a particularly good time for me, because something had been trying to spoil my day earlier. In this way, God took me back to grace. We ended up praising and worshipping together, and they both yielded themselves to the Lord. If I did not obey the promptings of the Lord, none of that would have happened. If I had delayed in my obedience, I might not have met them at that house. Open up for the promptings of the Lord and be ready to act as instructed, for there is an opportunity provided by grace.

The Need for Repentance

The New Testament starts out with the introduction of this new prophet, John the Baptist, who went about preaching that men everywhere should repent of their sins. Shortly after that, He baptized Jesus, who became another proclaimer of the same message. Repent, for the kingdom is here. The message was loud and powerful; men had to repent or an end was simply inevitable. When the day of Pentecost fully came, the Holy Spirit descended upon the disciples, and they began to announce the good news of the kingdom, saying, "Repent, and you shall be saved." To repent is to settle within you that the past is gone, and behold, you will start a new life in God.

We often use the phrase "give your life to Jesus," which, though not present in the Bible in exact words, delivers the same meaning and results in obtaining salvation. If you have repented and/or given your life to Jesus, you need to enhance your relationship with the Lord by going to a Bible-believing church. The Bible says:

Jesus answered and said unto him, Verily, verily, I say unto thee, Except a man be born again, he cannot see the kingdom of God. **John 3:3**

Repent ye, and believe the gospel. **Mark 1:15**

Many Christians make their appeal about going to church, instead of making it about repentance.

On the Day of Pentecost, Peter preached:

Repent, and be baptized every one of you in the name of Jesus Christ for the remission of sins, and ye shall receive the gift of the Holy Ghost. **Acts 2:38**

John the Baptist had also come, preaching that men should repent:

The Timing of God's Grace

In those days came John the Baptist, preaching in the wilderness of Judaea, and saying, Repent ye: for the kingdom of heaven is at hand. **Matthew 3:1-2**

Repentance is a requirement for salvation. In that first chapter of Galatians, Paul wrote:

But I certify you, brethren, that the gospel which was preached of me is not after man. For I neither received it of man, neither was I taught it, but by the revelation of Jesus Christ. **Galatians 1:11-12**

This gospel of grace came to Paul "by revelation." He continued:

For ye have heard of my conversation in time past in the Jews' religion, how that beyond measure I persecuted the church of God, and wasted it: and profited in the Jews' religion above many my equals in my own nation, being more exceedingly zealous of the traditions of my fathers. **Galatians 1:13-14**

Because this is the way Paul had been taught, he persecuted Christians and thought he was doing God a favor. Then something happened to him that changed everything:

But when it pleased God, who separated me from my mother's womb, and called me by his grace, to reveal his Son in me, that I might preach him among the heathen; immediately I conferred not with flesh and blood. **Galatians 1:15-16**

In the fullness of time, Paul was called by God's grace, and here we see for the first time the importance of the timing of that grace. We'll get to talking about the timing of grace a little later, but first please notice that Paul was talking about himself, about his life, about his upbringing. It was known widely at the time that he was a dangerous persecutor of Christians. Paul went all the way, and brought Christians down wherever he could. Because he had grown up in the religion of his fathers, he was zealous for it. But God had a different plan for Paul's life, and in His time, grace came to the persecutor, and that changed everything. From that moment on, something entirely different began to happen in and through this man.

Formed with Purpose

God called and separated Paul when he was still in his mother's womb. The Creator formed and fashioned him with a great purpose in mind. In fact, even before Paul's mother had conceived him, God had already finished designing him and had already settled what his end would be. Although God had finished it all, none of these things seemed apparent to Paul or to those who knew him. When he grew up, he began to live a life that was a complete contradiction to everything that God had destined for him. He called himself the worst of the worst, the chief of sinners. This lifestyle continued until the timing of God's grace kicked in, and then it all suddenly and dramatically changed.

Paul's experiences account for his advanced knowledge on destiny, divine planning, and predestination, which are boiling topics among Christians today. Some have questioned if everything that is happening is destined to happen. There are no easy answers to such a question. Nevertheless, to everything under heaven, there is a time and a season—a gestation phase to every seed—and so, yes, everything is destined. God is not the author of all things that are, yet the laws that govern the workings of things render every man the reward of their actions; as long as Earth remains, seed time and harvest shall not cease.

The Seed

In the beginning, the man who was the center of creation fell into sin by yielding to the devil's gimmicks. This act of disobedience cost him the garden, added pain for women in childbearing, and created an Earth that would demand the man to toil before eating. The Lord God not only passed judgment on every participant to this treasonous act, but also released a history-altering word:

And I will put enmity between thee and the woman, and between thy seed and her seed; it shall bruise thy head, and thou shalt bruise his heel. **Genesis 3:15**

The important point to note here is: *It [the seed of the woman] shall bruise your head.* This prophetic word served notice to Satan regarding the events of the future but never mentioned with precision the time and manner of its fulfillment. The devil has since been on a rampage to eliminate every seed. Whenever a woman went into labor, Satan had to be worried that this seed might be "The Seed," creating a unique warfare for every woman regardless of age or ethnicity. Woman! Satan is after you. He wants to destroy you before your seed sees the light of day. Some of these attacks on women manifest as sexual molestation and slavery, barrenness, miscarriages and abortions, genital mutilations, male chauvinism, and the like.

Though this passage speaks principally of the coming Savior, He is coming to be the firstborn among many brethren. There is no telling who the next evangelist, prophet, apostle, teacher, pastor, music minister, Dorcas, Timothy, or Peter will be and do among these brethren. So brace yourself for the accomplishment of prophecy in your life. YOU SHALL LIVE AND NOT DIE, YOUR SEED SHALL THRIVE, AND THE KINGDOM OF GOD SHALL WIN! Grace! Grace! To you and yours in Jesus' name.

Never Minimize Your Current Existence

You are a major player in a big story—the establishment of the human race as sons and daughters of the Most High. We shall all serve in the capacity designed by the Master Architect until all things come together. Do not look low on your reason for being; there is more to you than meets the eye. The Lord is doing great things in your life and has set a season for manifestation; so wait upon your hour of visitation. The Bible shows that God knows how to start out small, and nothing that He begins goes to ruin.

Moses, born at the time of Pharaoh's decree to destroy all male children, was preserved because his parents saw a future, and they released him to the Nile. Though scheduled for destruction, he rather grew up in the very house of Pharaoh, who initiated the decree. How much more will God show forth His grace in YOUR life? If you can understand the timing of the grace of God in your life, then you will know that something will eventually explode because of your destiny.

All Things Work Together

When Jesus was born, the news of His birth spread round about; from the humble shepherds to the nobles from the East, the announcement went forth. A King is born! This report posed a threat to those in leadership at the time. Herod, for fear of the unknown, issued an order to kill all of the babies under two years old.

If you study this scripture, you will notice that all events surrounding the birth of Jesus happened to fulfill what prophecy foretold. Jesus survived because God spoke to Joseph in a dream to take Him and flee to Egypt. It is, therefore, safe to say, *"And we know that all things work together for good to them that love God, to them who are the called according to his purpose"* **(Romans 8:28).**

In Galatians 1, Paul introduces his letter to the believers by communicating to them what he knew about his calling and election. Knowing what you have been called to do—or the assignment over your life—births in you laser vision and a high sense of purpose. You have to know it, and then you have to walk in it. When you know that God loves you, it causes you to also walk in the reality of that love. Personalizing what you know not only affirms someone else's testimony of you, but also opens up to you the opportunity of owning the testimony. Birthing a revolution and a miraculous move of God is, therefore, a product of owning God's testimony about you. The grace of God, in its proper time, starts to do some incredible miracles in and for you that words can hardly express.

Coincidence or God's Timing

At this point, we shall dive into one of the most amazing stories of all times. It brings into focus the lives of Zachariah, Elizabeth, Mary, Joseph, John the Baptist, and Jesus.

During the rule of Herod, King of Judea, there was a priest assigned service in the regiment of Abijah. His name was Zachariah. His wife was descended from the daughters of Aaron. Her name was Elizabeth. Together they lived honorably before God, careful in keeping to the ways of the commandments and enjoying a clear conscience before God. But they were childless because Elizabeth could never conceive, and now they were quite old.

It so happened that as Zachariah was carrying out his priestly duties before God, working the shift assigned to his regiment, it came his own turn to enter the sanctuary of God and burn incense. The congregation was gathered and praying outside the Temple at the hour of the incense offering. Unannounced, an angel of God appeared just to the right of the altar of incense. Zachariah was paralyzed in fear. But the angel reassured him, "Don't fear, Zachariah. Your prayer has been heard. Elizabeth, your wife, will bear a son by you. You are to name him John. You're going to leap like a gazelle for joy, and not only you—many will delight in his birth. He'll achieve great stature with God.

"He'll drink neither wine nor beer. He'll be filled with the Holy Spirit from the moment he leaves his mother's womb. He will turn many sons and daughters of Israel back to their God. He will herald God's arrival in the style and strength of Elijah, soften the hearts of parents to children, and kindle devout understanding among hardened skeptics—he'll get the

people ready for God." Zachariah said to the angel, "Do you expect me to believe this? I'm an old man and my wife is an old woman." But the angel said, "I am Gabriel, the sentinel of God, sent especially to bring you this glad news. But because you won't believe me, you'll be unable to say a word until the day of your son's birth. Every word I've spoken to you will come true on time—God's time."

Meanwhile, the congregation waiting for Zachariah was getting restless, wondering what was keeping him so long in the sanctuary. When he came out and couldn't speak, they knew he had seen a vision. He continued speechless and had to use sign language with the people.

When the course of his priestly assignment was completed, he went back home. It wasn't long before his wife, Elizabeth, conceived. She went off by herself for five months, relishing her pregnancy. "So, this is how God acts to remedy my unfortunate condition!" she said.

This chain of events could only have been orchestrated by "Someone" who, with a wide-view angle, was capable of seeing everything at the same time. The birthing of Jesus was scheduled to happen at a particular time in history. The fullness of things coming together was narrowed down to all the players and circumstances all being at the right place and executing their roles in a clearly defined sequence. The first player is Zachariah, who, according to design, came from a family of priests and married a daughter of the house of Aaron. It was of utmost importance that this combination and couple be just right for the child to be birthed—John the Baptist. These two lived an exemplary life, typifying the nature of

God in all they did. Elizabeth was called barren, but God held that womb to birth no ordinary child.

What God Has Been Saying

I declare the Word of the Lord over you: "You have entered a season of goodness, mercy, and favor. Know and understand the season that is upon you; the timing of My grace, which is now." Yes, this is the time for God's grace in your life. *Something* has suddenly appeared that is beginning to reveal the truth of God, the reality of Jesus Christ, in another way, and you are wondering: *Have I heard this before? Did I know this before? Oh, God, what is going on here? I am changed, and transformed every day.* The reason for it is simple: It is the timing of His grace. Embrace it.

Grace's Boiling Point

When working with God, there is a tendency to wonder how long it will take for certain miracles to happen. This scenario seemed to be the case playing itself out as Saul of Tarsus persecuted the believers of the early church. Paul declared himself to have been called and separated from his mother's womb, but for years it seemed as though God was slack concerning His promises. The persecution of the church claimed lives with every passing day, though prayers and faith mirrored the practices of the early church. Paul (then Saul) went about killing God's people without remorse. Then, at a certain moment, grace came to a boiling point. Many believers had prayed against Saul's schemes, but their prayers seemed not to get grace to bear. Unbeknownst to them, God collected those prayers, even as the furnace of grace continued to heat up.

Churches believed in deliverance from Saul, but grace just kept on bubbling for Saul as he undertook his next mission: to kill the Christians of Damascus. Neither the praying Christians nor the team of persecutors under Saul's command knew this would be the last mission of the sort. It was while he was on his way to this mission that the pot finally boiled over:

And as he journeyed, he came near Damascus: and suddenly there shined round about him a light from heaven. **Acts 9:3**

When the grace of God shows up, stories are about to change. In this case, Saul's persecution of the church was about to come to a sudden halt. At a particular spot on the road, the Hand of God, together with timing, located the vessel of destiny, and transformation, as it were, suddenly erupted within Saul of Tarsus. Light from heaven struck Saul and threw him off his high horse, light so powerful he was blinded for a season. A powerful moment in history that brought together not only the answer to prayers and a seasonal halt to persecutions, but also a change of heart to the leading persecutor. Oh Lord Jesus, pour out more of Your grace. What a magnificent picture of God's grace and the timing of grace.

And now also the axe is laid unto the root of the trees: therefore every tree which bringeth not forth good fruit is hewn down, and cast into the fire. **Matthew 3:10**

It's time. The enemy's cup is full. The situation that has been keeping you down has run its course, and it is now the time for God's grace.

Believe For Your Shift With Me

At this point, we have come to a close on our study on God's ability working in, through, and around us, and I would like to join my faith with yours for an impending shift as we make this declaration.

It is now the timing for the grace of God in my life. Years may have passed, but my time has now come. I may have been jobless for a while, but this is my time. I may have been childless until now, but this is my time. I may have been living in poverty, but this is my time. I may have been suffering from other people insulting me and using me, but this is my time.

Though for some time I didn't see a way out, now, all of a sudden, the light of God has illuminated my path. Now I can see the errors that held me back, the mistakes that prevented me from moving forward. Every hidden and uncertain thing has now come to light because it is God's time. Light shines in the darkness, and darkness cannot comprehend it. This is my time. Everything that God has declared over my life is coming to pass. Therefore, I will lift up my hands and bless the name of the Lord. I worship You, Father. I give You glory, and I give You honor.

I thank You that Your grace has a timing, and when that timing comes to fullness, nothing can stop that which You desire to do. You have begun it, and now You are finishing it. This is the time; I shall not turn aside or frustrate Your grace in my life. I bless You, Father. I give You glory, and I give You honor. In the name of Jesus.

I remember, God, that You told Isaac not to move from his place, even though it was a time of famine. Everything looked dry, but Isaac obeyed You and sowed in the land of hunger, and the surprising result was that he received a hundredfold increase that same year. I believe that I will have a similar increase because I have waited for You, Lord; waited for the season of Your grace. I have waited for Your favor, Your goodness, and Your mercy.

Father, I thank You. I bless You, and I glorify You. I declare, even as You have spoken it, "This mountain shall become a plain. This mountain has become flattened. My financial mountains have become a level land. The mountain of curses has become a flat, in the name of Jesus. The mountain of poverty has become a plain. The mountain of jealousy has become flat land. The mountain of denial has become a plain. The mountain of rejection has become a plain. It has not happened by might or by power, but by Your Spirit, Lord."

Therefore, I can now shout, "Grace! Grace!" I bless You, Father. I give You glory and honor. I thank You for the reality of Your Word. And I receive what it teaches me about Your grace and the seasons of Your grace, and I will walk in it.

Thank You, Father, for goodness, mercy, and favor.

Thank You, Lord, in Jesus' name,

Amen!

Conclusion

There is a system called grace through which the yielded live, move, and have their being. This system is an energy field yet also a personality—God. In and through Him, all things consist. As a result, salvation, success, greatness, and achievement are not far-fetched concepts prepared for just a handful of persons.

You can do ALL things through Him. Set your mind on Him and His system; yield to the possibility that He can, and so you can and watch the magic at work within you. To the one who seeks Him and His Kingdom first shall all things be added. The pursuit of such a spiritual path yields untold possibilities to the seeker who through his actions is saying, "I shall reach out to the One who is greater than I am."

All things work together for my good: from the weather, bus drivers, police officers, the law, doctors, the weak, the strong, the angels and demons, the likable and the disliked. It is a conspiracy but a well-meaning one. The all-knowing Master Planner is orchestrating all things toward One Great End. The benefactors and big winners of this great system are those informed of its workings who endeavor to cooperate with the currents of its ever-flowing stream.

You are the center of your world, and all else works in collaboration with you to bring to pass the things designed by the great architect of all worlds—God. So without your presence and participation, NOTHING will happen! Jump in then and begin an incredible journey with GRACE!

Grace comes free of charge to people who do not deserve it and I am one of those people... Now I am trying in my own small way to pipe the tune of grace. I do so because I know, more surely than I know anything, that any pang of healing or forgiveness or goodness I have ever felt comes solely from the grace of God.

Philip Yancey

CPSIA information can be obtained
at www.ICGtesting.com
Printed in the USA
BVOW03s2255040917
493957BV00001B/75/P